GERMAN

TEXANA

A Bilingual Collection
of Traditional Materials

By Gilbert J. Jordan

EAKIN PRESS ★ BURNET, TEXAS

FIRST EDITION

Copyright © 1980
By Gilbert J. Jordan

Published in the United States of America
By Eakin Press, P.O. Box AG, Burnet, Texas 78611

ALL RIGHTS RESERVED

ISBN 0-89015-261-6

FOREWORD

My collecting of songs, poems, and other items of German cultural heritage began some years ago, and I have searched for, gathered, and recorded these traditional treasures for many years. Actually my interest in German-Texan culture goes back to my childhood in a bilingual community in Mason County, Texas, where German poems and songs were passed along by oral tradition at home and transmitted to the children in the school and the churches. To this day I can quote from memory some of these poems and songs.

Once I was convinced that there was a need for an anthology of German Texana, I intensified my search for these traditional materials. I added several areas, such as drinking songs and the old familiar songs current in German-Texan communities, and I extended the geographical area of searching. The results were gratifying, and my collection was greatly enriched by these additions. In order to reach the people who could furnish me with the poems and songs needed for my anthology, I asked some friends in the German Belt of Texas to help me find the people and the desired material. I also published appeals in local newspapers and ethnic journals, made trips to interview prospective informants, corresponded with the people, and sent out questionnaires.

While collecting the German Texana for the present volume, I was very fortunate in getting the assistance of knowledgeable German-speaking contributors. Texas still has a number of such people, and some of them have precious memories of their cultural heritage. Even some whose command of the German language is no longer flawless, can still recite poems, proverbs, anecdotes, riddles, and prayers, and sing German songs. My interviews turned out to be pleasant confessions and delightful, nostalgic meetings, as well as productive sessions. I found that these people, when properly motivated by someone they trust, can recall from memory long-forgotten bits of verse and songs, and they enjoy doing so. They gladly recited, dictated, or wrote down what they remembered; and I recorded these treasurers in writing.

Without the aid of these helpers, the collection would not have been possible. To be sure, many of the poems and songs are available in books, such as those listed in the bibliography, but I wanted to collect only such vernacular culture as the people in Texas still remembered. I used books primarily to corroborate the oral versions I heard, to fill in a few spots where my informants could not remember some lines or words, and to get exact texts of the familiar songs I quote.

To those who helped with the collection—either orally or in writing—I am very grateful. The names of these contributors with short biographical information appear in the appendix and their initials in the text of the anthology along with the items they contributed or verified. In cases where several individuals gave different versions or parts of a song or poem, I list more than one source; and when I received several duplicates I often record only the first respondent. As might be expected, there are a number of alternate versions for some of the material, and I included some of these variants.

It was clear to me from the beginning that no matter how much material I gathered, all of it must be translated into appropriate English verse, as nearly identical with the original as possible. This then became one of my chief concerns, and translating the familiar verse turned out to be both challenging and rewarding.

In translating the German poems, songs, and ditties, I had to decide in a few cases whether it was preferable to keep the literal meaning and perhaps come up with a prosy, non-poetical form, or to keep the original flavor of the verse. In most cases I managed to keep both the basic meanings as well as the poetic sytle, which in some instances is just as revealing and always more charming than any word-for-word rendition could be. Almost always I managed to keep the meter and the rhyme of the original. This makes it possible to sing the translated songs to their familiar tunes. Melody notes for some of the songs are included.

The words *German Texana* may seem incongruous, but they are not contradictory. The South-Central and West-Central areas of Texas were settled to a great extent by German immigrants in the nineteenth and twentieth centuries. These colonists brought with them a great treasure of German lore that has been kept alive and, in some cases, modified by the settlers and their descendants during the one hundred and twenty-five years residence in Texas. This lore is, of course, basically German, not Texan, but inasmuch as it has been acclimatized, modified, and transmitted in Texas, we are justified in calling it Texana. It is as much Texan as most of the English and American folksongs that are referred to as Texas folk songs, despite the fact that they might more appropriately be called English and American folksongs of Texas.

Actually there is very little Texas folklore, either English or German, but there are indeed local adaptations and variants of the European lore. This holds true for German as well as English traditional materials. Instances of adaptations, variations, and local Texan lore will be pointed out in the several chapters below. The best area for discovering indigenous German Texana is in the realm of bilingual stories and anecdotes that grew out of linguistic misunderstandings, in some gravestone inscriptions, and perhaps in a few autograph-album verses.

Throughout the book, expository comments and explanations are given wherever they might be helpful and necessary for the understanding of the various entries. Also musical notes for some of the songs are added to give the melodies of songs that may not be familiar to some readers. And finally, for all the verse entries, the author-collector's English rhymed translations are placed by the side of the original German texts, thus making a truly useful bilingual anthology.

Some of the poems, songs, prayers, ditties, proverbs, riddles, and anecdotes of the present volume appeared in the author's book *Yesterday in the Texas Hill Country* (Texas A & M University Press, College Station, Texas, 1979). Permission for using this material in the *German Texana* book was granted by the Press. Some of the items also appeared in the *Perkins Journal* 31, (S.M.U., Dallas, Spring, 1978): 1-21; in the *Rice University Studies* 63, (Houston, Summer, 1977): 59-71; and in the recent volume *German Culture in Texas,* edited by Glen E. Lich and Dona Reeves (Twayne Publishers, Boston, 1980): 176-188. All these publications also obtained permission from the Texas A & M University Press.

ABOUT THE AUTHOR

Gilbert J. Jordan is a native of Mason County, Texas. Here he spent his youth on a ranch in the Hill Country in the northwestern part of the German Belt. He attended a bilingual rural school and a German Methodist church. His ancestors came from Germany in the mid-nineteenth century and settled first in Comal and Gillespie Counties and later moved to Mason County. His experiences in a German-Texan community during the first quarter of the present century are beautifully described in his book *Yesterday in the Texas Hill Country*. Minute details about the family, community, school, church, and town give an "exact account of a life that is gone—so true that you can see the colors, hear the voices, smell the smells, and feel the sweat," as William D. Bedell writes in the *Houston Post*.

With this background, Jordan was ideally suited for collecting, editing, and translating the material of the present book. This collection of traditional cultural possessions in the German-Texan settlements represents a priceless treasure that was brought to Texas from abroad, and was acclimatized and preserved in south-central Texas. The time has come now for us to record such material while some of the elderly bearers of this cache of poems, songs, ditties, riddles, proverbs, prayers, and anecdotes are still with us. This is the purpose of the present book of German Texana.

Gilbert Jordan was prepared for a career of teaching, scholarship, and writing. He holds the B.A. degree from Southwestern University, the M.A. from the University of Texas, and the Ph.D. from Ohio State University. After several years of teaching in the public schools of Texas, he became Professor of German at Southern Methodist University, where he taught from 1930 until his retirement in 1968. Then he took a professorship at Sam Houston State University for an additional five years.

He has published extensively—magazine articles, essays, and books—in his field of German language and literature, as well as books on family history, poems, and a verse translation of Friedrich Schiller's *Wilhelm Tell*. After his second retirement he has been engaged in research and writing magazine articles and books in the field of German Texana.

CONTENTS

Foreword iii
1. Verses from Autograph Albums (Poesie-Alben) 1
2. Nursery Rhymes 13
3. School Book Verses and Rhymes for Older Children 22
4. Christmas and New Year's Songs and Verses 35
5. Hymns 43
6. Prayers, Blessings, and Religious Verse 53
7. Epitaphs in Verse Form 59
8. Traditional and Familiar Songs 77
9. Drinking Songs 100
10. Humorous Poems and Light Verse 109
11. Nonsensical Ditties and Tongue Twisters 118
12. Proverbs, Admonitions, and Picturesque Expressions 124
13. Riddles 136
14. Anecdotes and Jokes 140
Afterword 145
Bibliography 147
Appendix 149
Index of First Lines and Titles 155

1.

VERSES FROM AUTOGRAPH ALBUMS (POESIE-ALBEN)

German-Texan memory books or autograph albums, frequently adorned with ribbons and with floral designs, represent a venerable tradition in South-central Texas. In the early days the messages were written in the old unique German handwriting, and they contain verses and mottoes inscribed by friends and relatives. Sometimes floral emblems, called *Stammbuchblümchen* (album flowerlets), were pasted on the pages by the writers to accompany the verses, mottoes, and signatures. These emblems were also used on friendship cards, where they were glued on at one end of the card so that they could be raised up to reveal the name of the giver. These lacy floral stickers are similar to those used in Germany, and they have verses like these: "A token of love," "From a fond heart, faithful and true," "Life bear for you its sweetest flowers," "God's blessing upon you," "To the keeper of my heart," "Your life be bright," "May flowerlets of love / Around thee be twined / And the sunshine of peace / Shed its joys o'er thy mind," and many similar ones. Also a few German album flowerlets appear in some booklets, like *Innigen Glückwunsch*.

Girls sometimes also fastened curls tied with ribbons or small wreaths of braided hair to the pages by the side of their verses and names. The New Braunfels Sophienburg Museum contains several well preserved specimens of albums with such personal additions and ornaments.

These autograph books are similar to the German *Poesie-Alben*, (poetry albums). Friends and members of a family, especially girls, wrote verses and inscribed their names. The writers also tried sometimes to show their individuality by artistic signatures and bold flourishes. However, the most important part of the entries were the verses. These poems are the cultural heritage that has come down to us, and this is the material that is included in the present chapter.

Some of the verses are repeated from time to time, but there is an amazing variety of them. I have personally processed hundreds of

TITLE page from Cornelie Lungkwitz' autograph album, Fredericksburg. —*Photo, courtesy of Liesel Van der Stucken, San Antonio, and J.P.M., Institute of Texan Cultures, San Antonio, 1979.*

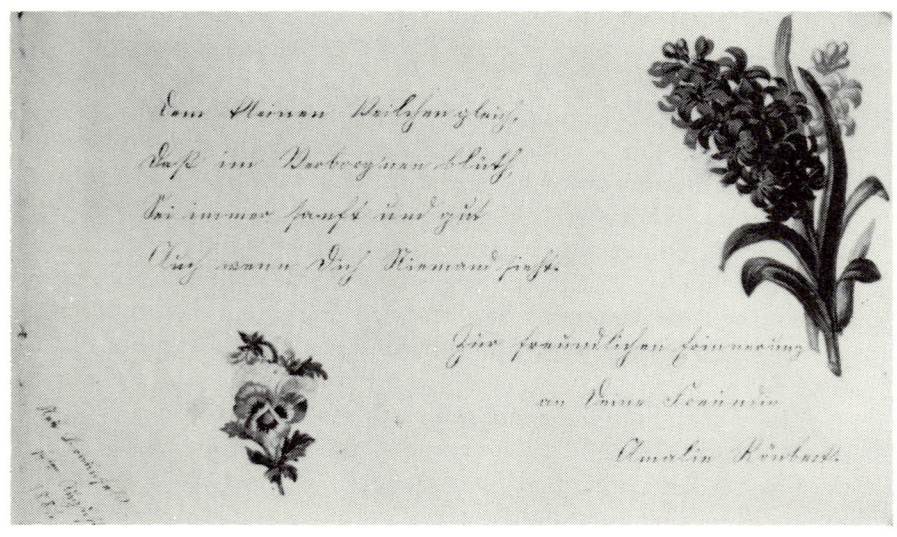

POEM and floral emblems from Elsa Groos' Autograph album, New Braunfels. Inscribed in 1881 by Amalie Rönbeck. The text is the same as No. 3 (Dina Jordan's album).
—*Photo, courtesy of M.W.*

different verses and I translated many of them into English verse, and at that my collection is but a small portion of the extant poems, some apparently written from memory. Others were composed locally or adapted from extant versions, but the majority were, no doubt, copied from books of album verses (*Verse für das Poesie-Album*), anthologies, hymnals, the Bible, and from other albums, many of which were brought to Texas by the immigrants. Such books are still in print (see Bibliography) but the search for the old sources and the linking of the Texas-German albums with those written in Germany, Switzerland, and Austria remains as a specialized study for the future. Suffice it to say here that there are direct relationships between the European and the Texan albums and album-verse books.

We might also mention that some of the extant albums have both German and English poems. Perhaps a few of the participants wanted to demonstrate their command of English, even though their mastery of the language was still a bit shaky, as the following ditty shows: "Friendship, love and walk so true / Ever walks beside of you." This ditty comes from New Braunfels and was contributed by R.H. The typical English verses were also adopted soon, and we find familiar lines like "Your album is a golden spot / To write in it: Forget me not." In general, the English and German poems are similar, but they have their own flavor, particularly the sentimental German verse with its recurring themes of love, friendship, nature, flowers, joy, piety, happiness, peace, beauty, loyalty, nostalgia, serenity, solitude, heartache, remembrance, hope, and trust.

To keep from having to give many long references, I chose to group the poems and their sources by counties of origin and list the respective contributors of each group. Then I record the individual poems and their writers as numbered entries.

MASON COUNTY. Collected for me by H.J.D., E.E.J., and H.K.P.

1.

Für dies kurze Menschenleben
Ist die Freundschaft viel zu schön;
Ewigkeiten muss es geben,
Wo sich Freunde wiedersehn.

For this fleeting human life
Is our friendship far too fair;
So eternity must be,
Where good friends will meet and share.

Minna Willmann, no date, in Hulda Jordan's album.

2.

Die Liebe gibt Freude,
Der Glaube gibt Ruh';
Drum wähle sie beide
Und glücklich bist du.
    Zum Andenken an deinen
        Cousin,
Friedrich Willmann, 1902, in Dina Jordan's album.

Love brings you joy;
Faith gives you peace;
So choose them both,
And your happiness won't cease.

    In remembrance of your cousin.

3.

Dem kleinen Veilchen gleich,
Das im Verborgnen blüht,
Sei immer fromm und gut,
Auch wenn dich niemand sieht.
    Deine Mama, Emilie Jordan.
In Dina Jordan's album.

Like a little violet
That blooms in secrecy,
Be pious and be good,
Though unseen you may be.
    Your mother . . .

4.

Ich dachte hin, ich dachte her,
Was wohl für dich das beste wär',
Da fiel der schöne Spruch mir ein,

Dina, du sollst glücklich sein!
Deine Freundin, L. Klett, no date, in Dina Jordan's album.

I thought of this and thought of that,
What for you would be the very best,
And then the happy thought struck me:
Dina shall be glad and blest.
    Your friend . . .

5.

Dich leite durch's Leben
Ein freundlicher Stern,
Der Glaube, die Liebe,
Der Friede des Herrn.
    Zum Andeken an deine Schwester,
Anna Jordan, January 8, 1902, in Dina Jordan's album.

May a friendly star
And faith and love
Guide you through life,
And peace from above.
    In remembrance of your sister . . .

6.

Das beste Glück sei dir beschieden,
So wandle froh durchs Leben hin;
In deinem Herzen wohne Frieden,
Auch sei für mich ein Plätzchen drin.
Emilie Schuessler Starks, no date, in Olga Tatsch Bauer's album.

May happiness to you be given,
May all your life be filled with glee;
May peace reside within your heart,
And may there be a place for me.

7.

Wenn des Lebens Stürme toben,
Wenn das Herz vor Kummer bricht,
Wende dich getrost nach oben,
Gott, der Herr verlässt dich nicht.

Hulda Lang, Castell, 1906, in Olga Tatsch Bauer's album.

When the storms of life are raging,
And your heart may break from care,
Turn your thoughts upward to heaven;
God will all your troubles share.

8.

So wie die Rosen blühen,
So blüh auch stets dein Glück,
Und wenn sie einst vergehen,
So denk' an mich zurück.

Adele Leifeste, 1907, in Olga Tatsch Bauer's album.

Just as the roses are growing,
So may your happiness grow;
And when some day they wither,
May your thoughts of me be aglow.

9.

Rosen blühen weiss und roth,
Liebe dich bis in den Todt,
Wahre Liebe endet nicht,
Bis der Tod das Leben bricht.
　Zum Andenken an deine Schwester,
Hulda Grote.

In Lydia Hoerster Kothmann's Album.

Roses blossom red and white;
I love you truly with all my might.
Love that's true will never break
Till death at last our lives will take.
　In remembrance of your sister.

10.

Trennen uns jetzt ferne Orte,
So behalte dennoch lieb,
Dessen Hand diese Worte
In dein Stammbuch niederschrieb.

A.H. Willmann. In Lydia Hoerster Kothmann's Album.

Though far apart in distant climes,
Keep dear in your heart the friend
Who wrote in happy times
These words near your album's end.

COMAL COUNTY (NEW BRAUNFELS). Collected by C.E.S.

11.

Felsen wanken, Eisen bricht,
Aber unsere Freundschaft nicht.
　Deine Freundin, Sophie Falke, 1855.

In Auguste Wiegreffe, nee Ervendberg's album.

Cliffs may fall, and iron break,
But our friendship will not quake.
　Your friend . . .

12.

Dein Leben sei fröhlich und heiter,
Kein Leiden betrübe dein Herz,
Das Glück sei stets dein Begleiter,
Nie drücke dich Kummer und Schmerz.
Dieses wünscht deine dich liebende
Freundin

Alwina Eichenroth, Hortontown, 1855. In Auguste Wiegreffe, nee Ervendberg's album.

May your life be happy and cheerful,
And no sorrow come over your heart;
May good fortune abide with you always,
May worry ne'er pain impart.
   This is the wish of your loving friend...

13.

Heiter nahe sich dir jeder Morgen,
Immer strahle dir der Freude Licht,
Frei von Ungemach und bangen Sorgen,
Lebe glücklich und Vergiss mein nicht.

Otillie Buchfeld, ca. 1890.

May each morning be for you serene,
May the light of joy e'er be your lot;
Free from hardship and devoid of worry,
Live happily and forget me not.

14.

Ich soll in dein Stammbuch schreiben

Und ich weiss nicht was.
Wir wollen gute Freundinnen bleiben.
Wie gefällt dir das?
   Deine Freundin Katie Schwab,

Solms (Comal County), April 17, 1897.

You want me to write in your memory book,
And I don't know just what.
We'll be good friends for ever more.

And how do you like that?
   Your friend . . .

15.

Ein Herz, was redlich denkt,
Braucht nicht viel zu schreiben;
Schreibt ein Wort, das heisst:
Wollen uns immer treue bleiben.
   Zum Andenken an deine Schwester

Emma Donnerberg, ca. 1890's.

A heart, sincere and true,
Will write short words and few;
The words it says declare:
We'll be forever true.
   In remembrance of your sister . . .

16.

Wenn Felsen und Berge
Uns auch trennen, und ich
Nicht seh' mehr dich
So nimm nur Tinte und Feder
Und schreibe eine Zeile an mich.
   Zur Erinnerung an Deine Freundin,

Margaretha Fey, ca. 1890.

When cliffs and mountains, high,
Keep us apart, and I
No longer can be nigh,
Then take your pen and try
To write a few lines to me.
   In remembrance of your friend . . .

17.

Geniesse stets der Jugend Freuden
Mit heiterem Gesicht,
Und trifft dich auch ein kleines Leiden,
So sei es kurz wie dies Gedicht.

Zur Erinnerung von Louise W., 1890's.

Enjoy the pleasures of your youth
Forever with a cheerful face;
And should some sorrow ever strike you,
May it be short just like this verse.
    In remembrance of . . .

18.

Lebe glücklich, lebe froh,
Wie die Maus in Hafer Stroh.

Deine Freundin, Ella Kirchner, ca. 1890.

Live happily and be gay
Like a mouse in the oats and hay.
    Your friend . . .

19.

Wenn du einst nach vielen Jahren
Dieses Werkchen wirst durchlesen,
So denk wie froh wir waren,
Als wir Kinder noch gewesen
Und mit frohem, heiterm Sinn
Gingen nach der Schule hin.

Zur Erinnerung an deine Freundin, Alma Paulus, 1896.

When some day after many years
You will read this booklet through,
Just think how happy we were when
We were children, I and you,
And with happy, cheerful minds
Went to school together then.
    In remembrance of your friend . . .

20.

Voraus sind mir alle die andern,
Drum muss ich auf den Deckel wandern.
Doch wenn ich auch nicht vorne bin,

So bin ich doch im Album drin.

Zum Andenken, Deine Cousine Paula, 1894.

The others took up every nook,
So I must write on the cover of the book,
And though I'm not on the pages inside,
I will within your album abide.
    In remembrance of your cousin . . .

A FRIENDSHIP card, ca. 1900. The floral designs were also pasted into some autograph albums.

KENDALL COUNTY (SISTERDALE AND COMFORT).
Transcribed for me by A.W.P.

21.

Nichts soll deine Tage trüben,	May your days ne'er fill with sadness,
Immer sei dein Leben schön,	Ever be your lifeline fair,
Und bei denen, die dich lieben,	And with those who love in gladness
Soll gewiss mein Name sein.	May my name in mem'ries share.

Adele Langbein Bausch, 1899, in Anna Poss' album.

22.

Trennen uns einst viele Meilen	If some day we are far apart
Unter Mond- und Sonnenschein,	Beneath the light of moon and sun,
So sollen diese wenigen Zeilen	May these few lines be in your heart
Ein Denkmal unsrer Freundschaft sein.	And tell of friendship well begun.

Ludwine Langbein Oelkers, 1899, in Anna Poss' album.

23.

O, wie ist es doch so schön,	Oh, how nice it always is
Wenn sich zwei Cousinen lieben,	When two cousins their love can share,
Immerhin sich gerne haben,	Or at least their fondness show,
Niemals sich betrüben.	And cause no sadness and no care.

Frida Fischer Schwope, 1899, in Anna Poss' album.

24.

Unter Palmen silber Kränzen	Under a silver palm tree wreath
Soll dein Name ewig glänzen,	Shall your memory ever breathe;
Ewig fromm und ewig rein,	Always faithful and always pure
Du sollst meine Freundin auf ewig sein.	Shall our friendship e'er endure.

Otto Behr, 1898, in Anna Poss' album.

25.

Dein Glück sei gross;	Your happiness be great
Dein Leiden klein;	Your suffering be small;
So sollen meine Wünsche sein.	So shall my wishes e'er be all.

Louise Ebell Haag, 1899, in Anna Poss' album.

26.

Ruhe wohn' in deiner Seele,
Freundlich lächle dir das Glück,
Und in deinem Leben fehle
Nie ein heitrer Augenblick.
Hedwig Langbein Scheele, 1899, in Anna Poss' album.

May peace within your soul abide,
May happiness upon you shine
And never turn from you aside,
And cheerfulness and joy combine.

27.

Wenn du einst in frohen Stunden
Mit der Augen hellen Blick
Dieses Blättchen hast gefunden,
O, so denk an mich zurück.
Amanda Behr Habenicht, 1900, in Anna Poss' album.

When in happy hours some day
With your bright eyes you will find
This slip of paper on life's way,
Oh, keep me ever in your mind.

28.

Wer sich an andere hält,
Dem wankt die Welt;
Wer auf sich selber ruht,
Steht gut.
Ottmar E. Fischer, 1900, in Anna Poss' album.

Whoever on others will depend,
His world is shaky and soon will end;
Whoever depends upon his own,
He stands as solid as a stone.

29.

Fest wie ein Fels im Meer
Soll unsere Freundschaft stehn,
Dann wird in unserem Zelt
Ein heil'ger Frieden wehn.
Bertha Ebell Schlater, 1899, in Anna Poss' album.

Firm as a rock in the sea,
Shall ever our friendship stand;
Then in our tent will be
The sacred peace of the land.

30.

Verbanne, verscheuche, verjage die Sorgen,
Sei heiter am Abend und heiter am Morgen,
Und denke zuweilen mit heiterem Blick
An deine dich liebende Tante zurück.
Jenny Behr Fischer, 1899, in Anna Poss' album.

Dispell, drive away, dislodge all worry,
Be happy in the evening, be happy in the morning,
And think sometimes with a look of cheer
Of your loving, adoring auntie, dear.

31.

So wie das Veilchen im Moose,
Bescheiden, sittsam und fein,
Doch nicht wie die stolze Rose,
Die nur bewundert will sein.
Paula Behr Treiber, 1899, in Anna Poss' album.

Be like the violet in the moss,
Discreet and modest and kind,
But not like a proud, proud rose,
That to admiration is inclined.

32.

Zufrieden sein ist grosse Kunst,
Zufrieden scheinen, grosser Dunst,
Zufrieden werden, grosses Glück,
Zufrieden bleiben, Meisterstück.
Bertha Bauer, 1900, in Anna Poss' album.

To be contented is an art,
To seem contented falls ever short,
Becoming contented is sheer increase
To stay contented is a masterpiece.

33.

Weil ich der Kleinste bin,
Schreib' ich ganz hinten hin.
(Quoted from memory by I.I.P.)

Because I am the smallest one,
I'll write in back and quickly run.

34.

The first line of the following verse is written on a line sloping uphill and the second, on a line going down hill.

So geht's bergauf,
So geht's bergunter;
Wenn du deine Freunde zählst,
So zähle mich darunter.
(Quoted orally and illustrated by I.I.P.)

This goes uphill,
And this goes down;
When you count your friends,
Don't let me down.

GUADALUPE COUNTY (ZORN AND YORK'S CREEK). Transcribed by R.H.

35.

Freunde sind wir stets gewesen,
Lange haben wir uns gekannt.
Wirst du dieses Blättchen lesen,
Gedenke deiner Freundin Hand.
Katherine Strempel, York's Creek, 1885, in Anna Ruehle's "The Golden Floral Album."

We have ever been good friends,
Long has been our friendship here.
When you read this slip of paper,
Think of me, your friend, so dear.

36.

Die Erde Kann vergehen,
Die Sonne kann verblassen,
Doch wahre Freundschaft
Soll uns nie verlassen.

The earth may pass away,
The sun may cool and fade,
But friendship, true, will stay;
So do not be afraid.
      In remembrance of your cousin . . .

Zur Erinnerung an deinen Vetter Gustave Dietert, York's Creek, 1883, in Anna Ruehle's "The Golden Floral Album."

37.

Wer ein Wort der Freundschaft hegt,
Braucht nicht gar viel zu schreiben.
Er spricht ein Wort, das heisst,
Wir wollen Freunde bleiben.

Whoever harbors words of friendship
He need not write much and clever;
He'll speak the words that say:
"We will be friends forever."
      In remembrance of your friend . . .

Zur Erinnerung an deine Freundin Mary Wisian, ca. 1880's, in Anna Ruehle's "The Golden Floral Album."

38.

Ruhig sollst du in der Ferne
Nach dem blauen Himmel schauen,
Wo dir leuchten die drei Sterne:
Hoffnung, Liebe und Vertrauen.

In the far-away, above,
In the heavens, blue and fair.
Your three stars are shining there:
Trust and hope and constant love.
      In remembrance of . . .

Zur Erinnerung an Anna Mehlitz, York's Creek, 1883, in Anna Ruehle's "The Golden Floral Album."

39.

Rosen und Vergissmeinnicht
Sind die besten Gaben;
Emma hat sie abgepflückt,
Anna soll sie haben.

Forget-me-nots and roses
Are gifts we treasure high;
Emma plucked them and discloses:
Anna gets them bye and bye.
      In happy remembrance of . . .

Zur fröhlichen Erinnerung, Emma Bierstedt, York's Creek, 1883, in Anna Ruehle's "The Golden Floral Album."

40.

Jedes Herz, das Freunde findet,
Ist beglückt, bleibt ewig jung;
Und wenn endlich alles schwindet,
Bleibt ihm die Erinnerung.

Every heart that finds some friends
Is happy and stays young and true;
When all else at last then ends,
My memory will stay with you.
   In friendly remembrance of . . .

Zur freundlichen Errinnerung an Olga Fuermann, in Anna Ruehle's "The Golden Floral Album."

41.

Freundschaft, edle Himmelsblume,
Die das Leben uns versüsst,
Die im stillen Heiligtume
Unsere Herzen mild erschliesst.

Friendship, noble heavenly bloom,
Which makes sweet our life on earth,
And in every sacred room
Opens up our hearts in mirth.
   In remembrance of your cousin . . .

Zur Erinnerung, Cousine Bertha Dietert, York's Creek, 1885, in Anna Ruehle's "The Golden Floral Album."

42.

Stets sei dein Schicksal sanft und milde,
Dein Leben Wonne, Glück und Heil,
Dein Pfad ein lachend Lustgebilde,
Und die Zufriedenheit dein Teil.

May your fate be mild and gentle,

May your life be full of bliss,
And your path be filled with gladness.
Satisfaction be your share of this.

Deine Freundin, Anatonia Eberhard, in Anna Ruehle's "The Golden Floral Album."

Your friend . . .

As can be seen from the above specimens of autograph-album verses, the poems reveal a fairly even poetic quality, indicating that most or all of them were taken from printed sources and adapted to individual situations as needed.

In the next two chapters we shall turn to children's verses and generally known school-book poems.

2.

NURSERY RHYMES

Children's literature, both English and German, has grown to enormous proportions in the present century. However, we are not concerned here with the recent literary productions, but instead with the older traditional verses, like those recorded in the English "Mother Goose" volumes and the German collections by Arnim and Brentano, and the Brothers Grimm. Parents and teacher taught these poems and songs to the children, and the verses were usually transmitted orally. Some also reached the pages of the elementary school readers, but most of them are more suitable for pre-school children.

There is actually very little or no native Texas lore of this type, and we may safely assume that the poems and the minor variations on the familiar themes originated in Germany long ago and were brought to Texas by the immigrants. The minor variants probably resulted from the lack of printed sources. The people had large families, so there were abundant opportunities to recite or sing the verses and transmit them to the children. Many of the verses were known as songs, and the melodies are well known in Texas. Notes are available for most of the songs.

Children's poems are frequently associated with play activities, such as counting-out games, like the English "Eeny-meeny-miney mo" or "one, two, buckle my shoe." Others are finger counting games, like "This little pig went to market," hand-patting games like "Patty cake, patty cake, baker's man," knee-bouncing exercises, like "This is the way the lady rides," pain-easing songs, verses for swinging, and lullabies. For the present chapter the poems are grouped roughly in the above-named categories.

COUNTING-OUT VERSES

1.

Eins, zwei, drei, vier, fünf, sechs, sieben,	One, two, three, four, five, six, seven,
Meine Mutter kochte Rüben,	My mother cooked turnips in the oven,
Meine Mutter kockte Speck,	Mother cooked the bacon slow,
Ich oder du musst weg.	Either I or you must go.
(A.E. & D.A.J.)	

Variant:

Eins, zwei, drei, vier, fünf, sechs, sieben,	One, two, three, four, five, six, seven,
Eine alte Frau kockt Rüben,	One old woman cooks turnips in the oven,
Eine alte Frau kocht Speck,	One old woman cooks bacon slow,
Und du gehst weg.	And now you must go.
(D.T.J.)	

2.

Eins, zwei, drei, vier, fünf, sechs,	One, two, three, four, five, six,
Im Hof ging eine alte Hex,	Out in the yard was an old witch,
Sie brummte immer hin und her,	She growled around the yard out there,
Sie brummte wie ein alter Bär.	She growled just like an angry bear.
(C.E.S. & A.E.)	

FINGER-COUNTING GAMES (*FINGERSPIELE*)

3.

These verses are spoken as you touch the fingers, one by one, from the thumb to the small finger.

Dies ist der Daumen,	This is the thumb,
Der schüttelt die Pflaumen,	He shakes down the plum,
Der hebt (löst, rafft) sie auf,	This one picks them up,
Der bringt (trägt) sie nach Haus,	This one takes them home to sup,
Der frisst sie alle auf.	This one eats them all up.

Variant:

Der kleine Schelm frisst sie alle auf.	The little one eats them all alone.
(M.L. & W.L.)	

4.

Der ist in den Busch gegangen,	This one went into the bush,
Der hat ein Häschen gefangen,	This one caught the rabbit,
Der hat es heimgebracht,	This one brought him home to eat,
Der hat es gebraten,	This one fried him for a treat,
Der Kleine hat alles aufgegessen.	The little one ate all the meat.
(D.A.J. & A.E.)	

5.

The following verse accompanies a slightly different game. While the first couplet is spoken, you draw a circle with your finger on the child's forehead. For the second couplet you touch the bridge of his nose, and for the last you pinch or tickle his chin.

Hier ist eine Maus,	Here is a mouse;
Die baut sich ein Haus.	She builds herself a house.
Hier ist eine Mück',	Here is a midge;
Die baut sich eine Brück'.	She builds herself a bridge.
Hier ist ein Floh,	Here is a flea;
Der macht so.	He does this to me.
(H.W.)	

A HAND-PATTING GAME

6.

Speak or sing the following verse while you teach the child to pat his hands together, as in the English "patty cake" ditty.

Backe, backe Kuchen!	Baking, baking cookie!
Der Bäcker hat gerufen:	The baker man is calling:
Wer will guten Kuchen backen,	Who would bake a tasty cake
Der muss haben sieben Sachen:	Seven things he has to take:
Eier und Schmalz	Eggs and lard,
Zucker und Salz,	Sugar and salt,
Milch und Mehl,	Milk and flour,
Safran macht den Kuchen gehl (gelb),	Saffron makes the cake turn yellow,
Schieb in den Ofen 'nein!	Shove it in through the oven door.
(E.W.K. & H.J.D.)	

KNEE-BOUNCING GAMES

In the following games the parent lets the child ride on a knee or on a swaying foot, bouncing the child up and down or back and forth, and finally pretending to let him fall.

7.

There are two other stanzas to the following poem, but they are not well known in Texas:

Hopp, hopp, hopp!	Trot, trot, trot,
Pferdchen, lauf Galopp,	Horsie, run a lot,
Über Stock und über Steinchen,	Over sticks and over stonies,
Pferdchen, brich dir nur kein Beinchen.	Do not fall and break you bonies,
Hopp, hopp, hopp, hopp, hopp,	Trot, trot, trot, trot, trot!
Pferdchen lauf Galopp!	Horsie, run a lot.
(C.E.S. & I.I.P.)	

There are variant readings of lines three and four, substituting *Steine* (stones) for the diminutive *Steinchen* (stonies), and *Pferdchen, brich dir nicht die Beine* for *Pferdchen, brich dir nur kein Beinchen.* (D.A.J.)

8.

Wenn die Kinder kleine sein,	When the kids are small and wee,
Reiten sie auf Stöckelein;	A stick horse will their horsie be;
Wenn sie grösser werden,	When they're big and stronger,
Reiten sie auf Pferden.	They'll ride their horses longer.
Dann geht das Pferdchen tripp und trab,	Then the horse goes pit-a-pat
Und schmeisst den kleinen Reiter ab,	And throws the rider tit-for-tat,
Plumps! Da liegt er unten.	Bump! He hits the bottom.

(F.J.)

(NOTE: A good variant for line two is: *Reiten sie auf Vaters Bein.* (D.A.J. & I.I.P.) (They'll ride on Papa's leg.)

9.

Here is an interesting alternate to No. 8. It shows a native German flavor with its reference to *Sachsen* (Saxony) and *Königs Schloss* (king's castle). It is not too well known in Texas.

Hopp, hopp, Reiterlein,	Trot, trot, little chap,
Wenn die Kinder kleine sein,	When the kids still need a nap,
Reiten sie auf Mutters Schoss	They will ride on Mama's lap.
Wenn sie grösser werden,	When they are big and stronger,
Reiten sie auf Pferden.	They'll ride their horses longer.
Wenn sie grösser wachsen,	And when they're big and grown,
Reiten sie nach Sachsen.	They'll ride away on their own.
Reiten vor des Königs Schloss,	They'll ride before the royal place,
Schiessen drei Pistolen los:	And shoot three pistols in the chase:
Piff, paff, puff!	Pow, pow, pow!

(A.E., I.I.P.)

10.

Galopp, galopp, Kartoffelsupp,	Galoup, galoup, potato soup,
Morgen kommt die Tante	Tomorrow comes our auntie
Mit ein'm Sack voll Leberwurst	With a sack of liverwurst
Für die Musikante.	For musicians, dandy.
(Für die ganze Bande.)	(For the whole gang.)

A variant for the last line reads: *"Dann muss der* (name of child) *tanze."* (J.H.K.) "Then must (*child's name*) dance."

11.

Hoppe, hoppe, Reiter;	Trotting, trotting, horseman,
Fällt er hin, so schreit er.	If he falls there's cursing.
Fällt er von dem Pferde,	If he falls around,
Liegt er auf der Erde.	He'll surely hit the ground.
Fällt er in das grüne Gras,	If he falls into green grass,
Macht er sich sein Pelzchen nass.	His little coat will be a mess.
Fällt er in den Sump,	If he falls into the marsh,
Macht der Reiter plump.	The little rider will go splash.
(D.T.J.)	

12.

Wie reiten die grossen Herren?	How do great gentlemen ride?
Ross, Ross, Ross.	Horses, horses, horses.
Wie reiten die jungen Herren?	How do young men ride?
Fass, Fass, Fass.	On barrels, barrels, barrels.
Wie reiten die Bauern?	How do poor peasants ride?
Klitter, klatter, klitter, klatter.	Chitter, chatter, chitter, chatter.
Bums, da liegt er im Graben.	Bump! He hits the bottom.
(R.K.E.)	

13.

For the first couplet of the following poem sway legs back and forth; for the second, trample feet; for the third, bounce up and down.

So fahren die Damen,	This is how the ladies drive,
So fahren die Damen.	This is how the ladies drive.
So fahren die Herren,	This is how the men drive,
So fahren die Herren.	This is how the men drive.
So schüttelt der Baum,	This is how the tree shakes,
So schüttelt der Baum.	This is how the tree shakes.
(B.C.S.)	

LULLABIES (*WIEGENLIEDER*).

14.

Eia, popeia,
Was raschelt im Stroh?
Es sind die kleinen Gänschen,
Die haben keine Schuh,
Der Schuster hat's Leder,
Keine Leisten dazu,
Kann er den Gänslein
Auch machen kein' Schuh'.
(E.W.J.)

Eia, popeia,
Who's scratching in the straw?
It is the little goslings,
They have no shoes and no paw.
The cobbler has leather,
But no lasts and no saw,
Can't make any shoes
For the goslings to lose.

NOTE: There are additional stanzas, but they are not known well in Texas.

15.

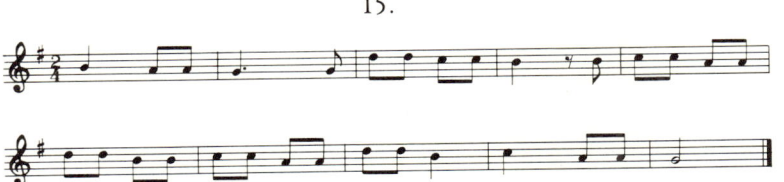

Schlaf, Kindchen, schlaf!
Der Vater hütet die Schaf',
Die Mutter hütet die Lämmerlein [das Kindelein]
Droben in dem Kämmerlein.

Sleep, Baby, sleep!
Your father is watching the sheep;
Your mother is watching the little room [lit., the little lambs]
Upstairs where Baby will slumber soon.

Schlaf, Kindchen, schlaf!

Sleep, Baby, sleep.

(NOTE: I remember only this first stanza, but other contributors furnished variants and additional verses, like those quoted below.)

Schlaf, Kindlein, schlaf!
Der Vater hütet die Schaf.
Die Mutter schüttelt's Bäumelein,
Da fällt herab ein Träumelein.

Sleep, Baby, sleep!
Your father is watching the sheep;
Your mother is shaking the little tree;
Sweet dreams fall down for you and me.

Schlaf, Kindlein, schlaf!
(D.T.J. & E.W.K.)

Sleep, Baby, sleep.

Schlaf, Kindlein (Kindchen), schlaf!
Am Himmel ziehn die Schaf.
Die Sternlein sind die Lämmerlein,
Der Mond, der ist das Schäferlein,
Schlaf, Kindlein, schlaf!

Sleep, Baby, sleep!
Up in the sky are sheep.
The stars are little lambs, so dear,
The moon, the shepherd, is so near.
Sleep, Baby, sleep.

(NOTE: There are various other stanzas, and the Arnim and Brentano *Wunderhorn* has a six-stanza version, 852-853. Below is an unusual pedagogical adaptation.)

Schlaf, Kindlein, schlaf,	Sleep, Baby, sleep!
Da draussen geh'n zwei Schaf',	Out yonder are two sheep.
Ein schwarzes und ein weisses;	The one is black, the other is white;
Und wenn das Kind nicht schlafen will,	And if you will not go to sleep,
Kommt das schwarze und beisst es.	The black one will come and bite.
Schlaf, Kindlein, schlaf!	Sleep, Baby, sleep.

(A.E.)

A PAIN-EASING SONG

16.

This little song is sung or spoken to a child who has some minor hurt, while the parent blows on the sore spot. The first two versions are very similar, and the first with the rain and mud is best known in Texas, while the second with its rain and snow is usually heard in Germany and in the North.

Heile, heile, Segen,	Healing, healing, blessing,
Drei Tage Regen,	Three days of rain,
Drei Tge Dreck,	Three days of mud,
Und jetzt ist alles weg.	And now there's no more pain.

(F.J. & D.A.J.)

The German snow version below is also known in Texas.

Heile, heile, Segen,	Healing, healing, blessing,
Morgen gibt es Regen,	Tomorrow it will rain,
Übermorgen Schnee,	The next day it will snow,
Und jetzt tut's nicht mehr weh.	And now there's no more pain.

(G.J.J.)

There is still another version known in Texas, and it is a cheerful variant.

Heile, heile, Segen,	Healing, healing, blessing,
Drei Tage Regen,	Three days of rain,
Drei Tage Sonnenschein,	Three days of sunshine,
Wird alles wieder heile sein.	And all is well again.

(D.T.J.)

THREE ADDITIONAL POEMS.

17.

Hin und her, her und hin,
So geht die Schaukel still und sacht.
Und es sitzt mein Püppchen drin,
Das gar hell vor Freude lacht.
(D.T.J.)

Back and forth, and to and fro
Goes the swing so soft and still,
And my doll goes high and low,
While she gaily laughs from thrill.

18.

The following is a short Texas version of a slightly longer poem sung in Germany. The short version given here is well known in Texas.

"Muh, muh, muh," so ruft die bunte Kuh.
Wir geben ihr das Futter;
Sie gibt uns Milch und Butter.
"Muh, muh, muh," so ruft die bunte Kuh.
(G.J.J.)

"Moo, moo, moo," so calls the pretty cow.
We give her feed and fodder;
She gives us milk and butter.
"Moo, moo, moo," so calls the pretty cow.

The German version usually reads:
". . . so ruft im Stall die Kuh."

". . . so calls in the stall the cow."

19.

Eins, zwei, drei,
Alt ist nicht neu,
Neu ist nicht alt,
Warm ist nicht kalt,
Kalt ist nicht warm,
Reich ist nicht arm,
Arm ist nicht reich,
Hart ist nicht weich,
Fleissig ist nicht faul,
Ein Kind ist kein Gaul.
(G.J.J.—See also A Warnemünde, *Thüringer Fibel*, 128)

One, two, three,
Old is not new,
New is not old,
Warm is not cold,
Cold is not warm,
Rich is not poor,
Poor is not rich,
Hard is not soft,
Busy is not lazy,
A child is no daisy.
(Literally "horse")

From these "Mother-Goose" type of poems for pre-school children, we turn next to rhymes for school children who could read the familiar verses in their elementary school readers.

3.

SCHOOL-BOOK VERSES AND RHYMES FOR OLDER CHILDREN

The present section includes material for slightly older children in the elementary grades. The children that had bilingual and bicultural education read and memorized these poems and songs in school. Most of the people who had this training in their childhood still know such verses by heart. Only those items remembered by one or more of the Texas informants are included in the present chapter. The texts of some of this material are found in the charming, old-fashioned eclectic readers and school books, like those by Fick, Weick, Grebner, and Bacon, all of which are listed in the bibliography. These books have become very rare because they are all out of print and most of them have not been used since World War I. The poems and songs were retained in the precious memories of the people and were transmitted to me orally or in writing. In those cases where the texts appear in the books, I compared the oral and the published versions, and I found either a great similarity or almost total agreement.

Also a number of poems and songs that do not appear in the books are included in the present chapter. Like the items in the school books, they are part of the lore preserved by the German ethnic group. This material was probably brought over from Germany by the oral tradition, though some of it surely existed in printed form, too. The material of the present chapter is presented in the following categories: poems about animals; poems of home and family; number ditties, counting-out, ball-bouncing and rope-jumping verses; alphabet rhymes; poems about the seasons; and miscellaneous poems.

MOTHER and daughter. A page from Weick & Grebner, *Deutsches Erstes Lesebuch* (German First Reader).

POEMS AND SONGS ABOUT ANIMALS.

1.

Häschen sass in grünen Gras,
Häschen dachte, "Was ist das?

Kommt dort nicht der Jäger her,
Bringt mit sich ein gross Gewehr?"
Husch, mein Häschen, husch,
In den dichten Busch!

Jäger zieht den Hahn schon auf—
Liebes Häschen, lauf doch, lauf!
Ach, jetzt legt er an und knallt,
Dass es durch die Büsche schallt'.

Schau, wie Häschen laufen kann,
Hat doch keine Stiefel an.
(M.M.J. & C.E.S.—See Weick, *Erstes Lesebuch*, 24-25.)

Rabbit sat in the grass, so green;
Rabbit thought: "What does this mean?

Isn't that the hunter's gun,
And it's time for me to run?"
Rush, my rabbit, rush
Into the thickest bush.

Hunter cocks his mighty gun;
Precious rabbit, run, oh run!
Now he aims; the gun goes "Boom!"
Through the bushes, spreading gloom.

But look how rabbit now can run
Without his boots, but it's no fun.

2.

Fuchs, du hast die Gans gestohlen,
Gib sie wieder her;
Sonst soll dich der Jäger holen
Mit dem Schiessgewehr.

Seine grosse, lange Flinte
Schiesst auf dich den Schrot,
Dass dich färbt die rote Tinte,
Und dann bist du tot.

Liebes Füchslein, lass dir raten,
Sei doch nur kein Dieb.
Nimm, du brauchst nicht Gänsebraten,
Mit der Maus vorlieb.
(H.J.D.—See Weick, *Zweites Lesebuch*)

Fox, you stole our big, fat goose,
Bring her back right now,
Else the hunter shoots you down
With his gun: "Pow, pow!"

With his big and mighty rifle
Shoots you in the head;
You'll get colored red with blood,
And you will be dead.

Foxy, dear, you'd better hear,
Do not be a thief.
You don't need roast goose, instead
Eat a mouse, you thief.

3.

Wer meine Gans gestohlen hat,
Der ist ein Dieb;
Wer mir sie aber wiederbringt,
Den hab' ich lieb.
(A.E. & D.T.J.)

Whoever stole my good old goose
He is a thief indeed.
Whoever brings her back to me
He is a friend in need.

4.

Kommt ein Vogel geflogen;
Setzt sich nieder auf mein'n Fuss;
Hat ein'n Zettel im Schnabel
Von der Mutter einen Gruss.
(G.J.J.)
Variants:
Vom Schätzel einen Gruss, Vom
Dirndl einen Gruss.

Comes a birdie a flying,
And he sits on my feet;
In his beak is a greeting
From my mother so sweet.

From my sweetie (gal), so sweet.

5.

Grau, grau Mäuschen,
Bleib in deinem Häuschen!
Frisst du mir mein Butterbrot,
Kommt die Katz' und beisst dich tot.
Grau, grau Mäuschen,
Bleib in deinem Häuschen.
(A.E. & M.A.G.)

Gray, gray mousie,
Stay inside your housie.
If you eat my butter bread,
Comes the cat and bites you dead.
Gray, gray mousie,
Stay inside your housie.

6.

Alle meine Enten (Entchen)
Schwimmen auf dem See,
Kopf (Köpfchen) im Wasser,
Schwanz (Schwänzchen) in der Höh'.
(E.W.K., I.I.P., & D.A.J.)

All my little ducklings,
Swimming on the sea;
Their heads are in the water,
Their tails are all you see.

7.

Wenn Möpschen auch oft grämlich tut,
Dem Hänschen ist es immer gut.
(NOTE: Möpschen is a dog.)
(D.T.J.)

Though Mopsy acts in an ugly way,
For little Jack it's all o.k.

8.

Ein Huhn und ein Hahn,
Die Predigt geht an;
Eine Kuh und ein Kalb,
Die Predigt ist halb;
Ein' Katz' und ein' Maus,
Die Predigt ist aus.
(F.J. & E.W.K.)

A rooster and a hen,
The sermon will begin;
A cow and a calf,
And that is just half;
A mouse and a cat,
It's over with that.

A second stanza is found in Arnim & Brentano, 824.

POEMS OF HOME AND FAMILY.

9.

Ich weiss, die Mama liebt mich,
Wie sie nur lieben kann;
Sie sagt's, und o, sie täuscht nicht,
Sie hat's noch nie getan.
(E.E.J.—See also Margaret & Meyer, 60, for the rest of the stanzas.)

I know my mama loves me,
As loves no other one;
She says so and deceives not;
This she has never done.

10.

Wenn du noch eine Mutter hast,
So danke Gott und sei zufrieden,
Nicht allen auf dem Erdenrund
Ist dieses hohe Glück beschieden.
Und hast du keine Mutter mehr,
Und kannst du sie nicht mehr bedrücken,
So kannst du doch ihr frühes Grab
Mit frischen Blumen Schmücken.
(H.W.)

If you still have a mother, dear,
Thank God for this and be content.
Not for all people on earth below
Is such good fortune always sent.
And if your mother is here no more,
And you can cause her no concern.

You still can decorate her grave,
With flowers, fresh, and fern.

11.

Hänschen klein geht allein
In die weite Welt hinein.
Stock und Hut steht ihm gut,
Ist gar wohlgemut.
Aber Mutter weinet sehr,
Hat ja nun kein Hänschen mehr.
"Wünsch ihm Glück," sagt ihr Blick,
"Kehr' nun bald zurück!"

Sieben Jahr', trüb und klar,
Hänschen in der Fremde war,
Da besinnt sich das Kind,
Kehret heim geschwind.
Doch nun ist's kein Hänschen mehr,
Nein, ein grosser Herr ist er,
Stirn und Hand, braun gebrannt,
Wird er wohl erkannt?

Eins, zwei, drei geh'n vorbei,
Wissen nicht, wer das wohl sei.
Schwester spricht: "Welch' Gesicht?"
Kennt den Bruder nicht,
Kommt dort rein sein Mütterlein,
Schaut ihm kaum ins Aug' hinein,
Ruft sie schon: "Hans, mein Sohn!"
"Grüss dich Gott, mein Sohn!"

(Variants have *Eilet* for *Kehret* in line 12; "*Braun gebrannt, Stirn und Hand,*" in line 15; and *Spricht* for *Ruft* in line 23.) (D.A.J., D.T.J. & A.E.)

Hänsel, small, not too tall,
Goes into the world alone,
Hat and cane are his gain,
Give him style and tone.
Mama cries and sheds a tear,
Now she has no Hänsel, dear.
"Wish him luck," says her glance,
"Come back soon, my Hans."

Seven years, good and bad,
Hänsel was away and glad,
Then this boy came home with joy,
Quickly came, but was coy.
Now he's not a little lad;
No, he's taller than his dad.
Face and hand, brown and tanned.
Who will know him in the land?

One, two, three pass by me;
No one knows who that might be.
Sister says: "Whose face is that?"
Knows her brother not,
Then his mother, dear, comes near.
When his eyes to her appear,
She cries out: "Oh, Hans, my son,
"May God bless you, Son."

Hin und Her

Ein Buch für die Kinder

Zusammengestellt von

H. H. Fick

SUPERVISOR OF GERMAN, CINCINNATI PUBLIC SCHOOLS

———

NEW YORK ∴ CINCINNATI ∴ CHICAGO
AMERICAN BOOK COMPANY

TITLE page of H.H. Fick, *Hin und Her.* See Bibliography.

NUMBER DITTIES, COUNTING-OUT, BALL-BOUNCING, AND ROPE-JUMPING RHYMES.

12.

Eins, zwei, drei, vier, fünf, sechs, sieben;	One, two, three, four, five, six, seven;
Wo ist denn mein Schatz geblieben?	Has my sweetheart gone to heaven?
Ist nicht hier, ist nicht da;	Is not here, is not there;
Ist wohl in Amerika.	Must be in America, fair.

(G.J.J. & H.W.)
(NOTE: The Fredericksburg version has *Herz*, heart, instead of *Schatz*, sweetheart.)

13.

This is a ball-bouncing ditty, like the English "One, two, buckle my shoe."

Eins, zwei; Polizei.	One, two; policemen do.
Drei, vier; Offizier.	Three, four; officers roar.
Fünf sechs; alte Hex'.	Five, six; mean old hex.
Sieben, acht; gute Nacht.	Seven, eight; Good night, it's late.
Neun, zehn; zu Bette gehn.	Nine, ten; let's go then. (Lit., go to bed)
Elf, zwölf; kommen die Wölf'.	Eleven, twelve; comes the wolf.

(D.T.J. & I.I.P.)

14.

Eins, zwei, drei, oder vier;	One, two, three, or four;
Mädel, wenn du tanzen willst,	Girlie, if you want to dance,
Dann komm und tanz mit mir.	Come and dance with me some more.
Fünf, sechs, sieben, oder acht;	Five, six, seven, eight;
Mädel, wenn du müde bist,	Girlie, if you're tired now,
Dann sage "Gute Nacht."	Say "Good Night"; it's late.

(T.K. & M.M.J.)

15.

Ene, dene, Tintenfass,	Eeny, meeny, inkwell glass,
Geh zur Schul' und lerne was.	Go to school and learn to pass.
Wenn du was gelernet hast,	When you've learned a thing or two,
Komm nach Haus und sag mir das.	Come and tell me, right and true.
Eins, zwei, drei; du bist frei.	One, two, three; you are free.

(D.T.J.)

16.

Ene, dene, Tintenfass,	Eeny, meeny, inkwell glass,
Tintenfass und Leder;	An inkwell and a feather (quill),
Tintenfässer sind aus Glas,	Inkwells are all made of glass.
Mappen sind aus Leder.	Letter cases are made of leather,
Leder kommt von Ochs und Kuh;	Leather comes from ox and cow,
Ochs und Kuh, die schreien "Muh."	Ox and cow are bawling now:
"Muh, muh, muh,"	"Moo, moo, moo,"
Der Ochs bist du.	The ox, that's you.

(A.B.S.)

17.

Ich und du und Müllers Kuh;	I and thou, and Miller's cow;
Bäckers Esel, das bist du.	Baker's donkey, that art thou.
A second line variant reads:	
"Des Metzgers Esel, das bist du."	Butcher's donkey, that art thou.

(G.J.J. & E.G.)

Other variants reverse the ownership of the *Kuh* and the *Esel*.

18.

The following ditty is similar to the English "Rich man, poor man, beggar man, thief, / Doctor, lawyer, merchant, chief." You touch the buttons on your coat or dress as you say the verses. The last button tells who you or your future husband will be.

Edelmann, Bedelmann (Bettelmann),	Nobleman, beggar man,
Doktor, Pastor;	Doctor and pastor,
König, Kaiser,	King or Kaiser,
Schweinemajor.	Or piggy master (literally *major*)

(*Bedelman,* version: M.M.J., *Bettelmann,* version: E.G. & A.E.)

ALPHABET RHYMES.

19.

A, B, C,
Die Katze lief im Schnee,
Und als sie wieder 'rauskam,
Da hatt' sie weisse Zeh'.
Variants for the last line:
Da hatt' sie weisse Hosen an.
Da hatt' sie weisse Schuhe an.
(H.J.D., E.J.M., G.J.J., H.W., W.L.)

M, N, O,
The cat ran in the snow;
And when she came out again,
She had a white toe.

She was wearing white pants.
She was wearing white shoes.

20.
Der Osterhas' (The Easter Rabbit)

A, a, a,
Der Osterhas' ist da.
E, e, e,
Wir füttern ihn, juchhe!
I, i, i,
Das schmeckt wie noch nie.
O, o, o,
Der Osterhas' ist froh,
U, u, u,
Er nickt uns freundlich zu.
(A.E. & E.G.)

A, a, a,
Easter rabbit comes today.
E, e, e,
We'll feed him well, oh gee!
I, i, i,
He likes our apple pie.
O, o, o,
He's happy, this I know.
U, u, u,
He smiles when this we do.

POEMS ABOUT THE SEASONS.

21.

Im Winter, wenn es frieret,
Im Winter, wenn es schneit,
Dann ist der Weg zur Schule
Fürwahr noch mal so weit.

In winter when it freezes,
In winter when it snows,
Then is the way to school
Twice farther, and it grows.

Und wenn der Kuckuck rufet,
Dann ist der Frühling da,
Dann ist der Weg zur Schule
Fürwahr noch mal so nah.

And when the cuckoo's calling,
Then springtime's here again;
Then is the way to school
Twice closer than it's been.

Wer aber gerne lernet,
Dem ist kein Weg zu fern;
Im Frühling, wie im Winter,
Geht er zur Schule gern.
(G.J.J.—See Fick, 12-13.)

For him who likes to study
It's never far to go,
In spring and in the winter
He's never late or slow.

22.

Winter, ade!	Winter, good-bye!
Scheiden tut weh,	Parting is nigh.
Aber dein Scheiden macht,	But your partings make
Dass mir das Herze lacht.	My heart to laugh and wake.
Winter, ade!	Winter, good-bye!
Winter, ade!	Winter, good-bye!
Scheiden tut weh.	Parting is nigh.
Gerne vergess' ich dein,	Gladly I'll you forget,
Kannst immer ferne sein.	Stay far away and fret.
Winter, ade!	Winter, good-bye!
Winter, ade!	Winter, good-bye!
Scheiden tut weh.	Parting is nigh.
Gehst du nicht bald nach Haus,	If you won't soon go home,
Lacht dich der Kuckuck aus.	Cuckoos will laugh and come.
Winter, ade!	Winter, good-bye!

(G.J.J. & F.J.—See Weick, *Erstes Lesebuch*, 53.)

23.

Der Mai ist gekommen,	May has come in,
Die Bäume schlagen aus,	The trees are budding out;
Da bleibe, wer Lust hat,	Let him who wishes
Mit Sorgen zu Haus.	Stay at home with his gout. (Literally, *cares.*)

(E.G. & G.J.J.—See Weick, *Erstes Lesebuch*, 67.)

MISCELLANEOUS POEMS.

24.

Frisch ans Werk und säume nicht!	Quick to work, and don't delay;
Arbeit ist die erste Pflicht.	Work is duty every day.
Fange du nur mutig an,	Just begin and toil with fun;
Frisch gewagt ist halb getan.	Well begun is almost done.

(D.A.J. & D.T.J.—See Weick, *Erstes Lesebuch*, 7.)

Variant for lines 1 and 2:

Frisch ans Werk und nicht gesäumt;	Quick to work and don't delay
Was im Weg liegt, weggeräumt!	What's in the way must clear away.

(E.G.)

25.

Die Zunge ist ein kleines Glied,	A little organ is the tongue,
Doch hat sie grosse Macht;	Its might is great and strong;
Hat manchem schon um Glück und Fried',	From many a one it took away
Um Ehr' und Freud' gebracht.	His joy and friends one day.
Drum merke stets auf jedes Wort,	Thus closely watch each word with grace
Das deine Zunge Spricht;	Your tongue may speak in beauty;
Beachte sorgsam Zeit und Ort:	Mark carefully the time and place,
Auch Schweigen ist oft Pflicht.	For silence, too, is duty.

(G.J.J., E.E.J.—See Weick, *Erstes Lesebuch,* 16-17.)

26.

Ich bin der Herr Pastor,	I am the little pastor,
Ich predig' euch was vor.	I preach about disaster;
Und wenn ich nicht mehr weiter kann,	And when I can go on no more,
Fang' ich wieder von vorne an.	I'll start again, just as before.

(H.W.)

27.

The following ditty is spoken by Thumbling in the cow's stomach in Grimm's "Thumbling's Travels" ("Tom Thumb"). The children read and memorized it in school and spoke it at home when they milked a cow.

Strip, strap, stroll;	Strip, strop, strull;
Ist der Eimer bald voll?	Will the bucket soon be full?

(J.H.K. & D.A.J.—See Weick *Drittes Lesebuch,* 109.)

28.

The following song is sung for a play-party game. A ring is placed on a long string, and the ends of the string are tied together to make a loop the size of the circle of players sitting on the floor. The players move their hands back and forth on the string and pass the ring along. The person who is "it" stays in the center of the circle and when the singing stops, he tries to guess who has the ring. If he guesses correctly, he joins the circle, and the person who had the ring is "it."

Ringlein, Ringlein, du musst wandern
Von dem einen zu dem andern.
O wie herrlich, O wie schön,
Ist's wenn Ringlein wandern gehn.
(M.M.J. & T.K.)
Variant for line two:
Von der einen Hand zur andern.
Variant for line four:
Ringlein, du musst weitergehn.
(E.G. & D.T.J.)

Ringlet, ringlet, you must wander
From one person to another.
Oh, how splendid, oh, how nice
'Tis when ringlets wander farther.

From one hand into another.

Ringlet, you must wander farther.

    The songs presented above make up a delightful group of lyrics and poems that became a part of the people's cultural heritage. They are not so much folklore as they are a semi-literary tradition. Be that as it may, these verses became a vital part of the life in the German settlements.

A SAMPLE of German script. From Weick & Grebner, *Deutsches Erstes Lesebuch*. See text on page 32, No. 23.

4.

CHRISTMAS AND NEW YEAR'S SONGS AND VERSE.

German Christmas songs, like "Silent Night" and "Oh, Christmas Tree," have long been the common possession of both the German- and the Anglo-Texans, and they are sung in translation so much now that some people do not realize the original compositions are German, and some of these versions are almost forgotten now, even by the descendants of the German settlers. But under the awakening interest in the several ethnic cultures of Texas, the old German songs are coming to light again. In the present chapter I will quote the songs that are most familiar to the people in the German Belt of South Texas, along with other songs and poems not well known among English-speaking people. All will be accompanied by new English verse translations.

The familiar English version of "Silent Night" found in American song books is quite freely translated in spots, but it is adequate and generally accepted, in spite of the fact that it does not relate perfectly to the original. Actually three German versions were known in Texas, each with several stanzas, and all were sung to the familiar tune by Franz Gruber. It seems that at one time the various German churches favored and used one of these three versions, as evidenced by their inclusion in the hymnals. Only the first stanza of each of the three versions appears below.

1.

Here is the first stanza of the original Josef Mohr version as it has come down to us.

Stille Nacht, heilige Nacht!	Silent night, holy night,
Alles schläft, einsam wacht	All's asleep; by lone starlight
Nur das traute, hochheilige Paar.	Wakes the dear and holy pair
Holder Knabe im lockigen Haar,	O'er the boy with curly hair,
Schlaf in himmlischer Ruh',	Sleep in heavenly peace,
Schlaf in himmlischer Ruh'.	Sleep in heavenly peace.

(M.M.J. & T.K.—See Bacon, 134.)

The next version starts with the Mohr lines, but then varies at least in the wording, if not too much in meaning.

Stille Nacht, heilige Nacht!	Silent night, holy night,
Alles schläft. Einsam wacht	All's asleep, by lone starlight
Nur das heilige Elternpaar,	Wakes the holy couple alone,
Das im Stalle zu Behtlehem war,	Where the star of Bethlehem shone
Bei dem himmlischen Kind,	By the heavenly child,
Bei dem himmlischen Kind.	By the heavenly child.

Schmidt, 115—Zimmerman's version of line three reads:

Nur das fromme so heilige Paar	Only the pious and holy couple.

(E.G. & M.A.G.)

The third version seems to have been favored by the German-American Methodists, as evidenced by its inclusion in their hymnal (Nast, 108).

Stille Nacht, heilige Nacht!	Silent night, holy night,
Land und Meer ruht umher.	Land and sea calm will be.
Durch gebrochene Wolken von fern	Through broken clouds we see from afar
Glänzt der Heil verkündene Stern,	The redemption proclaiming, saving star,
Wo der Erlöser erschien,	Where our redeemer was born,
Wo der Erlöser erschien.	Where our redeemer was born.

(D.A.J. & M.A.G.)

2.

O du selige, o du fröhliche,
Gnadenbringende Weihnachtszeit!
Welt ging verloren,
Christ ward geboren:
Freue, freue dich, O Christenheit.
(D.T.J. & R.H.—See Nast. 99.)
One variant reverses the first two phrases and reads:
O du fröhliche, O du selige.

Oh thou blessèd, oh thou joyful,
Mercy-bringing Christmastide!
Lost were all people,
Christ came to save us:
Oh, rejoice ye, all Christendom.

3.

O Tannenbaum, O Tannenbaum,
Wie treu sind deine Blätter!
(Repeat both lines.)
Du grünst nicht nur zur Sommerzeit
Doch auch im Winter, wenn es schneit.

Oh Christmas tree, oh Christmas tree,
How faithful are your needles!
(Repeat both lines.)
Not only green in summertime,
But also in freezing wintertime.

O Tannenbaum, O Tannenbaum,
Wie treu sind deine Blätter.
(C.E.S. & W.L.—See Bacon, 132-133.)

Oh Christmas tree, oh Christmas tree,
How faithful are your needles.

4.

It was customary in some families for the children to stand around the Christmas tree and sing the song below before receiving their Christmas gifts, which lay or stood, unwrapped, by the decorated and lighted tree.

Der Chritbaum ist der schönste Baum,
Den wir auf Erden kennen;
Im Garten klein, im engsten Raum,
Wie lieblich blüht der Wunderbaum,

Wenn seine Blümlein brennen,
Wenn seine Blümlein brennen,
Ja, brennen.
(E.J.M., G.J.J.—See Liebhart, 21.)

The Christ-tree is the fairest tree
That we on earth can know.
In the smallest rooms our eyes can see
How lovely blooms the wondrous tree,

With its fiery blossoms glowing,
With its fiery blossoms glowing,
Yes, glowing.

5.

Alle Jahre wieder
Kommt das Christuskind,
Auf die Erde nieder,
Wo wir Menschen sind.
(G.J.J. & C.E.S.—See Schmidt, 114.)

Every year returning,
Comes the Christ child, dear,
Down to earth below
Where we humans are.

6.

Ihr Kinderlein, kommet, O kommet doch all',
Zur Krippe her kommet in Bethlehems Stall,
Und seht, was in dieser hochheiligen Nacht
Der Vater im Himmel für Freude uns macht.

O seht in der Krippe, im nächtlichen Stall,
Seht hier bei des Lichtleins hell glänzendem Strahl,
In reinlichen Windeln das himmlische Kind,
Viel schöner und heller, als Engel es sind.

Da liegt es, O Kinder, auf Heu und auf Stroh;
Maria und Joseph betrachten es froh,
Die redlichen Hirten knie'n betend davor,
Hoch oben schwebt jubelnd der Engelein Chor.

O beugt, wie die Hirten, anbetend die Knie,
Erhebet die Hände und danket wie sie,
Stimmt freudig, ihr Kinder, wer wollt' sich nicht freu'n?
Stimmt freudig zum Jubel der Engel mit ein!
(E.G. & E.W.K.—See Schmidt, 112.)

Ye children, oh come ye, oh come ye now all,
To the manger come over to Bethlehem's stall,
And see what in this holy, heavenly night
Our Father in heaven brings joy and delight.

Oh, see yonder manger, the stable by night,
See here by the lamplight now shining so bright,
All wrapped and protected the Heavenly Child.
Far fairer than angels, so tender and mild.

There lies He, oh children, on straw and on hay,
And Mary and Joseph admire Him all day;
The shepherds, so honest, kneel praying nearby,
While angels rejoice and sing praises on high.

Oh, bend ye your knees like the shepherds and pray,
And raise up your hands and give thanks just as they,
And join them in singing; who now could be sad?
Join happily in, and rejoice, and be glad.

7.

Morgen kommt der Weihnachtsmann,	Tomorrow comes old Santa Claus,

Morgen kommt der Weihnachtsmann,
Kommt mit seinen Gaben.
Trommel, Pfeifen und Gewehr,
Fahn' und Säbel und noch mehr,
Ja, ein ganzes Kriegesheer
Möcht' ich gerne haben.

Bring uns, lieber Weihnachtsmann,
Bring uns morgen, bringe
Musketier und Grenadier,
Zottelbär und Panthertier,
Ross und Esel, Schaf und Stier,
Lauter schöne Sachen.

Doch du weisst ja unsern Wunsch,
Kennst ja unsere Herzen.
Kinder, Vater und Mama,
Auch sogar der Grosspapa,
Alle, alle sind wir da,
Warten dein mit Schmerzen.
(E.W.K. & W.L.—See Schmidt, 114.)

Tomorrow comes old Santa Claus,
Comes with all his presents.
Drums and fifes and rifles, too,
Flags and sabers, and some more,
Yes, an entire army corps
I would like to have, now.

Bring us, dearest Santa Claus,
Bring tomorrow, bring us
Musketeers and grenadiers,
Teddy bears and panthers, too.
Horses, donkeys, sheep, and steers,
All these pretty playthings.

But you surely know our wishes,
And you know our hearts, too.
Children, Papa, and Mama,
Even dear old Grandpapa,
All of us, we all are here,
Waiting for your coming.

8.

Lieber Nikolaus,	Dearest Santa Claus,
Komm in unser Haus,	Come into our house,
Pack die Taschen aus!	Empty all your pockets out.
Alle Kinder essen gern	All the children like to eat
Äpfel, Nüsse Mandelkern.	Apples, nuts, and almonds, sweet.
(T.K. & A.E.)	

9.

Der Weihnachtsmann ist ein guter Mann;	Santa Claus is a good old man;
Er bringt den Kleinen, was er kann.	He brings the children all he can.
Die Grossen lässt er laufen;	The grown-ups he will leave alone;
Die könn'n sich selbst was kaufen.	They buy their presents on their own.
(G.J.J.)	

10.

Lieber, lieber Weihnachtsmann,	Dearest, dearest Santa Claus,
Sieh mich nicht so böse an!	Don't be angry in my house.
Stecke deine Rute ein!	Put your switch back in your sack;
Ich will immer recht brav sein.	I'll be good, so you'll come back.
(D.A.J.)	

11.

Morgen, Kinder, wird's was geben,	Tomorrow, children, things will happen,
Morgen werden wir uns freu'n,	Tomorrow will we happy be;
Welch ein Jubel, welch ein Leben	What merry making, what rejoicing
Wird in unsrem Hause sein.	Will we in our family see,
Einmal werden wir noch wach,	One more night, and you can say:
Heissa! dann ist's Weihnachtstag.	"Wow! this is our Christmas day."
(E.W.K. & C.E.S.)	

12.

There is also a Pentecost poem, similar to this New Year verse. See the chapter on Humorous Poems and Light Verse.

Wenn's Neujahr ist, wenn's Neujahr ist,	When New Year comes, when New Year comes,
Dann schiesst der Vater einen Bock,	Our father shoots a buck, so wild;
Dann tanzt die Mutter, dann tanzt die Mutter,	Then Mother dances, then Mother dances,
Dann fliegt der rote Rock.	And her red skirt twirls, my child.
(I.I.P. & R.H.)	

13.

At the New Year's celebrations some people gather and set off dynamite blasts to welcome the new year. Before the explosion someone speaks these lines:

Das alte Jahr ist verflossen;	The old year has passed away;
Das neue wird angeschossen.	We'll shoot in the new today.
(E.G.)	

The singing of the familiar German Christmas songs has always been an important tradition in the German-Texan communities, and the perpetuation of the songs is assured for the future, at least in their English translation. The German versions and the German poems, however, have fallen somewhat into disuse, and they might be forgotten before long, if it were not for their preservation on phonograph records and tapes. It is hoped that their inclusion in this book on German Texana will also aid in their preservation.

CHRISTMAS card with singing cherubs and candles, ca. 1910.

5.

HYMNS

In most German-Texan communities, except the freethinker settlements in Kendall County and elsewhere, the religious element was very strong and played a major role in the lives of the German immigrants and their descendants. One of the areas in which the church influence was most pronounced was in the singing of hymns. There were excellent church choirs, and all the people joined in the singing, raising their voices to make a joyful noise unto the Lord. Not only did they sing their songs in church; they sang at home while the family stood by a pump organ, and they sang the hymns while they worked on the farms and ranches or did the house work and cooking in the kitchen.

Considering the church-oriented lives of the people, it is no wonder that their hymns were one of the most positive and lasting features of the German element in the state. The songs were known so well, even memorized, that they were generally preserved better and longer than some other ethnic qualities.

Many of the church people can still sing these old hymns, and in several communities of the German Belt annual song festivals are held to the present day, for example in the Methodist churches of Mason, Art (Mason Co.), Hilda (Mason Co.), Castell (Llano Co.), and Monthalia (Gonzales Co.). Hundreds of people assemble on a certain Sunday afternoon each year at one of the former German churches and hold these hymn festivals. The people come from far and near and sing the old familiar songs in German, even though many of the younger participants are no longer completely conversant with the German language.

Some of the hymns that were sung in the old German churches especially in the German Methodist churches, were translations of English songs; and these, too, have lived on in the German communities. However, none of these songs is reproduced here, no matter how German the songs may seem to the German-Texans. These are English and Anglo-American hymns and for this reason are not exactly German Texana, although many of them have a real German flavor. The songs included here are original German songs. Some of them may have originated in the German-American churches, especially among the German Methodists, Mennonites, and the Moravian Brethern in the northern states, but they are also German. Although largely unknown in English, they represent some of the best and most favored songs sung in the German-Texan churches.

The present collection can be nothing more than a small sampling of the hundreds of German hymns that were sung by the various denominations in Texas, but they do represent a cross section of the hymns sung in the state.

1.

The following song was well known in most German Protestant churches. The German Methodists and the Lutherans used it extensively, often as a closing hymn. There is even an English translation by H. Brueckner in the *Service Book and Hymnal of the Lutheran Church in America,* 292. My translation reflects some influence of the Brueckner version.

Nimm, Jesu, meine Hände
Und führe mich,
Bis an mein selig Ende
Und ewiglich!
Ich kann allein nicht gehen,
Nicht einen Schritt.
Wo Du wirst geh'n und stehen,
Da nimm mich mit.

Oh, take my hands, dear Jesus,
And lead Thou me,
Until my bless'd departing
And eternally.
Alone I cannot wander
One single day;
Where Thou wilt guide my footsteps,
Take me along Thy way.

(D.J. & G.J.J.—See also Nast and Liebhart, 196.)

2.

Below is a hymn of blessing sung in the Lutheran and Evangelical Churches.

Herr, segne uns du,
Gib Frieden und Ruh',
Behüt' uns von allen Gefahren!

Lord, bless Thou us,
Give calm and peace,
Protect us from all danger.

Lass dein Angesicht
Mit himmlischem Licht
Und Freundlichkeit leuchten uns Kindern!

Let thy holy face
With heavenly grace
And friendliness shine for us children.

Dein Antlitz erheb'
Auf uns und beleb',
O heiliger Geist, unsere Seelen.

Your countenance raise
And revive us with praise,
Oh, Holy Spirit, revive us.

So werden wir dein
In Ewigkeit sein,
O Jesu, sag': Amen, ja Amen!
(C.E.S.—See Schmidt, 111.)

Then we'll be Thine,
Forever we pine.
Oh, Jesus, say: Amen, yes Amen.

3.

Here is a typical German Methodist hymn, sung to the tune of "Oh, Worship the King."

Mein Hirt ist der Herr,
Des bin ich so froh;
Denn niemand, wie Er,
Erbarmet sich so.
Es kann ja den Seelen,
Die Jesus regiert,
Kein Gutes je fehlen,
Der Herr ist mein Hirt!
(G.J.J. & E.E.J.—See Nast and Liebhart, 461.)

My shepherd the Lord,
Of this I'm so glad;
No one, only He,
Has mercy on me.
And nothing is wanting
For souls Jesus won;
No good ever faileth;
The Lord is my own.

4.

Here is a cheerful and optimistic Protestant young people's song.

Lasst die Herzen immer fröhlich
Und mit Dank erfüllet sein.
Denn der Vater in dem Himmel
Nennt uns seine Kinderlein.
Immer fröhlich, immer fröhlich,
Alle Tage Sonnenschein.
Voller Schönheit ist der Weg des Lebens,
Fröhlich lasst uns immer sein.
(E.E.J.—See Munz, 14.)

Let our hearts be always joyful
And be filled with thanks and cheer.
For our Father who's in heaven
Calls us all his children, dear.
Always joyful, always joyful,
Sunshine every day we see.
Full of beauty is life's pathway always,

Joyful may we ever be.

5.
A Methodist Sunday-school song.

Wir sind kleine Schnitter,	We are little reapers,
Mühen uns mit Fleiss;	Working hard with might;
Auf dem Ährenfelde	On the spreading grainfields
Blinkt es reif und weiss.	Gleams the harvest white.
Sturm and Regengüsse	Storm and rain and downpours
Machen uns nicht feig',	Do not overwhelm;
Denn wir sammeln Garben	We are gath'ring sheaves here
Für das Himmelreich.	For the heavenly realm.
Chor:	Refrain:
Mühe, Mühe ist der Schnitter Los;	Working, working is the reapers fate;
Mühe, Mühe, doch der Lohn ist gross.	Working, working, our reward in great.

(Repeat the last four lines of the stanza.)

(Repeat the last four lines of the stanza.)

(D.T.J.—See Margaret & Meyer, 9.)

6.
A song of refreshment and redemption popular among Methodists.

"Wasserströme will ich giessen,"
Spricht der Herr, "aufs dürre Land;
Kühlend sollen Quellen fliessen
In der Wüste heissem Sand.
Wo jetzt Wand'rer schmachtend zieh'n,
Soll ein Gottesgarten blüh'n."
(E.E.J.—See Nast and Liebhart, 660.)

"Streams of water I'll be pouring,"
Says the Lord, "on desert land;
Cooling springs will soon be flowing
O'er the desert's burning sand.
Where the trav'lers now are pining,
Will God's garden soon be shining."

7.

A Methodist camp meeting song, also sung in the Evangelical Church.

Ich weiss einen Strom, dessen herrliche Flut
Fliesst wunderbar stille durchs Land;

Doch strahlet und glänzt er wie feurige Glut,
Wem ist dieses Wasser bekannt?
Chor:
O, Seele, ich bitte dich komm!
Und such' diesen herrlichen Strom;
Sein Wasser fliesst frei und mächtiglich,
O glaub's, es fliesset für dich.
(H.J.D.—See Nast and Liebhart, 289.)

I know a river's glorious stream
Flows wondrously still through the land;

Yet it shines and glows in fiery gleam.
Who knows of this water's strand?
Refrain:
Oh, my soul, I ask thee to come,
And seek out this glorious stream;
Its water flows freely and strong;
Believe that it flows to redeem.

8.
A Lutheran, Evangelical and Methodist children's song.

Gott ist die Liebe;
Lässt mich erlösen;
Gott ist die Liebe;
Er liebt auch mich.
Drum sag' ich's noch einmal:
Gott ist die Liebe;
Gott ist die Liebe;
Er liebt auch mich.
(E.J.M.—See Munz, 86.)

God is all loving;
He would redeem me;
God is all loving;
He loves me too.
So I will repeat it:
God is all loving;
God is all loving;
He loves me too.

9.
A funeral song (Methodist and Evangelical).

In dem Himmel ist's wunderschön,
O, wie gerne möcht' ich dort steh'n,
Wo statt Kampf, Schmerz, und Hohn
Meiner wartet die Kron',
Wo ich darf meinen Heiland seh'n.
(G.J.J.—See Nast and Liebhart, 571.)

In heaven it is wondrously fair;
Oh, I yearn to be lifted there;
Instead of strife, pain, and scorn,
A crown will adorn,
And I'll see my dear Savior up there.

10.
Martin Luther's well known hymn is sung in most Protestant churches. The following is a composite translation, adapted from the versions in *The Lutheran Hymnal*, 262, and the Lutheran *Service Book and Hymnal*, combined with some phrasings of my own.

Ein' feste Burg ist unser Gott,
Ein' gute Wehr und Waffen,
Er hilft uns frei aus aller Not,
Die uns jetzt hat betroffen.
Der alt' böse Feind,
Mit Ernst er's jetzt meint.
Gross' Macht und viel List
Sein' grausam' Rüstung ist,
Auf Erd' ist nicht seinsgleichen.

A mighty fortress is our God,
A good defense and weapon;
He frees us from distress and need
That has us now o'ertaken
Our ancient, evil foe
Is bent on doing us woe;
With cunning and great might
He's armed for a dreadful fight;
On earth is not his equal.

Mit unser Macht ist nichts getan,

Wir sind gar bald verloren.
Es streit für uns der rechte Mann,
Den Gott hat selbst erkoren.
Fragst du, wer der ist?
Er heisst Jesus Christ,
Der Herr Zeboath,
Und ist kein ander' Gott.
Das Feld muss er behalten.
(H.W.—Printed in the *Evangelisch-Lutherisches Gesangbuch,* 247—See also Schmidt, 108.)

With our own might can naught be done,
We'll soon be lost, rejected;
But for us fights the Valiant One,
Whom God Himself elected.
Ask you who that might be?
Christ Jesus, it is He;
Lord Sabaoth his Name,
From age to age the same,
And He must win the battle.

11.

Evangelical and Lutheran closing hymn. Also used in Sunday schools. This is stanza 3 of the hymn *"Nun, Gott Lob es ist vollbracht."*

Unsern Ausgang segne Gott,
Unsern Eingang gleichermassen;
Segne unser täglich Brot,
Segne uns mit sel'gem Sterben
Und mach uns zu Himmelserben.
(C.E.S., T.H.E.—*Kirchengesangbuch,* No. 9.)

May God bless our going out;
And as well our coming back;
Bless our daily bread, we pray;
Bless whate'er we do today;
Bless us in our hour of dying;
Grant us our reward in heaven.

12.

The following hymn is universally known in the Catholic Church. There are nine verses. Here is the first.

Grosser Gott, wir loben Dich!
Vor Dir neigt die Erde sich,
Herr, wir preisen Deine Stärke!

Und bewundern Deine Werke!
Wie Du warst zu aller Zeit,
So bleibst Du in Ewigkeit.
(M.M.J.—See Hellebush, 198.)

Almighty God, we give Thee praise!
The earth before Thee bows and says:
"Lord, we praise Thy might and power

And marvel at Thy works this hour.
As Thou wert in days of yore,
Thus art Thou for evermore."

13.

Here is one of the familiar Catholic *Mutter-Gottes-Gesänge* (songs to the mother of God).

Maria zu lieben/Ist allzeit mein Sinn;
Hab' ihr mich verschrieben,/Ihr Diener ich bin.
Mein Herz, o Maria,/Brennt ewig zu dir,
Vor Liebe und Freude,/O himmlische Zier.
(M.M.J.—See also Hellebush, 151.)

Mary to love/is always my sigh,
I gave her my promise,/her servant am I.
My heart, oh Mary,/burns ever for Thee,
With love and with joy/your glory I see.

From these well known church songs and hymns we turn next to a consideration and presentation of other religious verses: poetic prayers, rhymed table blessings, and poems with a religious theme.

Psalter und Harfe.

Lieder und Melodien

für

Schule, Haus und gottesdienstlichen Gebrauch.

Bearbeitet

von

H. Liebhart.

Hitchcock & Walden:
Cincinnati, Chicago und St. Louis.
Nelson & Phillips:
New-York.

TITLE page from a German hymnal. See Bibliography under Liebhart.

6.

PRAYERS, BLESSINGS, AND RELIGIOUS VERSE

Prayers were an intrinsic part of the church-oriented German Texans. These people attended church services and Sunday school each Sunday; and prayers, even by lay members of the church, played an important role in the services. Many of the church groups, especially the pietistic German Methodists, also held mid-week prayer meetings in the homes of the people, and this brought prayers into the home life. So close was the connection between the family, the church, and religion, that daily devotionals, consisting of Bible readings and prayers, and sometimes hymn singing, were held in the homes twice each day, around the breakfast and supper table. For the most part, these prayers were self-composed and memorized, and they were strongly influenced by the prayers heard in the church services.

In addition to these family prayers, there were a number of versified table blessings, spoken without exception before every meal. Almost all of these blessings were memorized and spoken while the family members sat around the table with folded hands and bowed heads. Most individuals had their favorite table prayers, some of which were universally known.

Children were taught bed-time prayers in verse form, and these German verses have been retained in the minds of the people. The small children, even teenagers, spoke them aloud while kneeling beside their beds before retiring. The number of these prayers is not great, but they were widely used in Texas, the same as abroad in earlier times. As the children grew older, they were told to compose their own prayers to be spoken silently.

Religious poems, most of them pertaining to table blessings, prayers, and Bible readings, were known far and wide. The main purpose of these verses was to exhort and urge the people to give thanks to God and ask for His guidance. The prayers and the religious lyrics, along with the well known hymns, give a deep insight into the religious life and beliefs of the German-Texans.

CHILDREN'S BED-TIME PRAYERS.

1.

Lieber Gott, mach' mich fromm,
Dass ich zu Dir in'n Himmel komm'.
(D.A.J. & T.K.)

Dear God, let me pious be
That I may get to heaven with Thee.

2.

In the following prayer, there is a common alternation between the words *ist* (is) and *mach* (make) in line one. Some people think Protestants perfer *mach* and Catholics, *ist,* but this is not uniformly so. Also some versions have *mag* (may), instead of *soll* (shall) in line two.

Ich bin klein, mein Herz ist (mach) rein,
Soll (Mag) niemand drin wohnen, als Jesus allein.
(H.J.D., Meth.; H.W., Lutheran; T.K., Cath.)

I am small, my heart is (make) pure,
Shall (May) none there dwell, but Jesus for sure.

3.

An interesting non-church, freethinker version of Number 2, above, reads as follows:

Ich bin klein, mein Herz ist rein,
Niemand soll drin wohnen,
Als Mama und Papa allein.
(I.I.P.)

I am small, my heart is pure,
No one shall dwell there,
But Mama and Papa for sure.

4.

The next prayer is frequently shortened to the first two lines. There is a similar four-line version in Arnim and Brentano, 831.

Lieber Gott, ich bitte Dich,
Ein frommes Kind lass werden mich!
Sollt' ich aber das nicht werden,
So nimm mich lieber von der Erden
Und führ' mich in Dein Himmelreich,
Damit ich werd' den Engeln gleich!
(M.M.J. & E.G.)

Dear God, I beg of Thee,
A pious child let me be.
But if perhaps this cannot be,
Then take me from this earth to Thee,
And take me to Thy heavenly home
So that like angels I become.

5.

An unusual, ungrammatical prayer was apparently adapted from the first two lines of Number 4. The grammatical error is in the use of *mich* for *mir*, both meaning *me*. In Number 4 above the phrasing is correct. Since the two case forms are commonly confused in Texan German, the version below may have originated in the state.

Lieber Gott, ich bitte Dich,
Mach ein gutes Kind aus mich.
(G.G.G. presented this version in a paper delivered at the Symposium on Texas Germans in San Marcos in 1978.)

Dear God, I beg of Thee,
Make a good child of me.

6.

The well known poem by Luise Hensel has become a familiar prayer. For this purpose it is usually shortened to the first six lines. Below is a three stanza version.

Müde bin ich, geh' zur Ruh',
Schliesse meine Augen (Äuglein) zu;
Vater, lass die Augen dein
Über meinem Bette sein!

Tired am I, go to bed,
Close my eyes, lay down my head;
Father, let the eyes of Thine
O'er my resting place incline.

Hab' ich Unrecht heut' getan,
Sieh es, lieber Gott, nicht an!
Deine Gnad und Christi Blut
Machen allen Schaden gut.

If I've done some wrong today,
Take, dear Lord, my guilt away.
For Thy grace and Christ's shed blood
Repair all harm and make us good.

Alle, die mir sind verwandt,
Gott, lass ruhn in deiner Hand!
Alle Menschen, gross and klein,
Sollen dir befohlen sein.
(T.K. & E.W.K.)

Friends and kinsmen in the land,
Let them rest within Thy hand;
All the people, great and small,
To Thy care I give them all.

7.

Breit' aus die Flügel beide,
O, Jesu, meine Freude,
Und nimm dies Kücklein ein!
Will Satan es verschlingen,
So lass die Englein singen:
"Dies Kind soll unverletzet sein."
(E.G.)

Spread out Thy pinions o'er me,
Oh, Jesus, I adore Thee,
And take this baby chicken in.
If Satan would devour me,
Let Angels sing, o'erpower me:
"This child shall be unharmed by sin."

TABLE PRAYERS AND BLESSINGS.

8.

Segne, Vater, diese Speise,
Uns zur Kraft und Dir zum Preise!
(D.J., G.J.J., E.G.)

Bless, our Father, this our food,
For Thy glory and our good.

9.

Segne, Vater, was wir essen,
Lass uns Deiner nicht vergessen.
(R.H. & E.G.)

Bless, our Father, what we eat,
And let us Thee not forget.

10.

Komm, Herr Jesu, sei unser Gast
Und segne, was Du uns bescheret hast.
(E.W.J.)

Come, Lord Jesus, be our guest,
And let the food you gave be blest.

11.

Für Speis' und Trank
Dem Geber Dank.
(M.A.G.)

For food and drink
The Giver we thank.

12.

Für Speis' und Trank
Hab', liebster Jesu, Dank
(R.H.)
Variant:
Gott, Dir sei Dank
Für Speis' und Trank.
(R.H.)

For food and drink,
Dear Jesus, we thank.

Our God, we thank
For food and drink.

13.

O Herr, segne diese Gaben,
Die wir von Dir empfangen haben.
(T.K.)

Bless, oh Lord, these gifts we see,
That we have received from Thee.

14.

Herrgott, himmlischer Vater,
Segne uns und diese Deine Gaben,
Die wir durch deine Güte
Empfangen haben!
(R.H. & E.G.)

Lord God, heavenly Father,
Bless us and these gifts we see,
Which we through Thy goodness
Have received from Thee.

15.

Lieber Gott, ich bin Dein Gast;
Segne, was Du bescheret hast.
(A.E.)

Dear God, I am Thy guest;
Bless what Thou provided hast.

16.

The Kendall County freethinkers did not speak the usual blessings. Instead they said *Mahlzeit*, short for *Gesegnete Mahlzeit* (Wish you a blessed meal). (W.L.)

OTHER RELIGIOUS VERSE.

17.

Wer ohne Gebet zu Tische geht,

Wer ohne Gebet vom Tische aufsteht,

Der ist dem Ochs und Esel gleich,
Und kommt auch nicht ins Himmelreich.
(D.T.J.)

Who without prayer at the table will sup,

Who without prayer from the table gets up,

He's like an ox and a donkey, dumb,
And will never to the kingdom of heaven come.

18.

Ohne Gottes Geist und Wort
Geh' niemals aus deinem Hause fort.
(D.T.J.)

Without God's spirit and His word
Go never from your house abroad.

19.

Wer ohne Gott und ohne Gebet
Des Morgens früh vom Schlaf aufsteht,
Und Gottes Lob vergessen kann,
O weh, wie traurig fängt er an.
(H.J.D.)

Who without God and without prayer
Gets up to breathe the morning air,
Who can forget to praise his God,
How sad he is and what a clod.

20.

Wo keine Bibel ist im Haus,
Da sieht's gar öd' und traurig aus,
Da kehrt der böse Feind gern ein,
Da mag der liebe Gott nicht sein!
(D.T.J.)

When there's no Bible in the home,
Things look quite bleak and sad.
The evil one will come in soon,
And God won't stay and make you glad.

21.

Below is a specimen of the sort of verse found over doorways of homes in Germany. In Texas it found its way into the *Fredericksburg Home Kitchen Cook Book,* p. 7, and thus it enters into German Texana.

Gott schütze mein Heim,	May God protect my home,
Gott schütze mein Haus,	May God protect my house,
Viel Glück zieh herein	May joy, abundant, to me come,
Und keines hinaus.	And none go from this house.
(D.T.J.)	

The prayer-poems reproduced above comprise a special sort of cultural heritage that exerted a powerful influence upon the German-Texan immigrants and their descendants. Although much of the material is slowly fading from the memories of the people, the influence continues even after the German-language culture gradually shifts to an Anglo tradition. Outsiders coming to the Texas German Belt can easily detect this religious influence to this day in the communities with a German background.

STEEPLE of the Upper Willow Creek M.E. Church, South, at Plehweville. Sketch by Tony Bell, 1976.

7.

EPITAPHS IN VERSE FORM.

German verse inscriptions on tombstones in Texas were quite common in the nineteenth century and well into the twentieth. In spite of the decline of German in Texas after World War I, some German poetic epitaphs were carved as late as 1951, for example on the grave marker for Albert Arhelger in Comfort. These verses are usually engraved below the names of the deceased and their dates of birth and death. Occasionally the place of birth is also inscribed on the stone, especially if the person was foreign born. Unfortunately some of the older headstones are so badly deteriorated that some words are hard to read, but there still are literally hundreds and thousands of well preserved inscriptions in the German-Texas communities.

Nearly all the epitaphs are written in rhyming German verse, giving them a distinctive poetic quality. As epitaphs go, these German verses are fairly good. To be sure, some are extremely sentimental and lachrymose, but in spite of the mournful flavor, there is also a deep undertone of love, faith, and hope. This reveals not only German sentimentality, but also the strong family ties of the people and the influence of the church. There are many Biblical verses, both English and German, but these quotations will not be included here because they are already well known.

German verse epitaphs seem to be more common than the English, but they are not too different from them. Here are a few English verse inscriptions which may be compared with the German epitaphs below:

Rest, mother, rest in quiet sleep
While friends in sorrow o'er thee weep:
   (Eliza Shippman, in Nancy Smith Cemetery, Somervell Co., 1901.)

Sleep, my darling, take your rest,
God called you home. He thought it best.
   (Adele Louise McDonald, Boerne, 1923.)

DOUBLE tombstone for "Mutter" and "Vater" Lich. Note the shells mounted on concrete mounds. Comfort Cemetery, 1888 and 1921.
—*Photo, T.G.J., 1979.*

Remember, friends, as you pass by,
As you are now, so once was I,
As I am now, so you must be,
Prepare for death and follow me.
(John A. Naegelein, Castroville, 1867.)

In general there is not much originality in the verses, and there is some repetition, indicating that most of them were derived from printed sources or they were copied from other gravestones. Sometimes the distance between cemeteries containing identical epitaphs is great, and this points to printed sources. A good example is the use of an inscription in the Cypress Mills Cemetery in Blanco County that is identical with one in the Round Grove cemetery in Denton County. (See Epitaph No. 26 below.) One of the best instances of an original epitaph is the one for Lucia Scheel (No. 6).

An in-depth study of the various German-Texas cemeteries—never mind the pun—would indeed be interesting from the standpoint of cultural heritage, but this is not the time or place for such research. Suffice it to say that by and large the cemeteries are well kept. Some of the early private burial plots are enclosed by sturdy stone walls, and in some of the public or church graveyards the individual family plots are also surrounded by similar walls. Some of the tombstones are large and imposing, but most of the older markers with the poetic inscriptions are quite modest. More unusual are the wooden and wrought-iron markers, some with inscriptions cast in raised letters on the metal.

In addition to the many poetic inscriptions—some in the old German or Gothic letters—the most striking features of the German-Texan cemeteries are the many carved or engraved symbols. In addition to the universally known crosses, lambs, doves, and clasped hands, there are some unusual symbols, like six-pointed stars, hearts, and stylized flowers, all carved in stone or wrought in iron. One of the extant wooden crosses even has hearts cut out at the top of the cross and on the two ends of the cross piece. Shells or remains of shells are another feature of the earlier grave mounds. Although the meaning of these pre-Christian symbols could not have been known in nineteenth-century Texas, shells were commonly pressed onto the earth of the mounds and later affixed to the concrete mounds or slabs.

The collection below is probably typical enough. In most cases, the location of the cemetery, the names of the persons, and the death or burial dates are included. Further study would probably reveal special features of the verse in Catholic and Protestant cemeteries, but no such attempt is made here.

CHILDREN'S EPITAPHS

1.

Er war ein stilles gutes Kind,
Fromm wie Gottes Engel sind.

He was a good and quiet child,
Like Angels in heaven, pious and mild.

Herbert K. Pape, New Braunfels, 1895-1895, also George R. Dukes, Boerne, 1892-1911.

2.

Vater, wenn die Mutter fragt,
Wo ist unser Liebling hin,
Wenn sie weint und um mich klagt,
Sag ihr, dass ich im Himmel bin.

Father, when my mother asks,
Where has our dear darling gone?
When she cries for me, then tell
That I've gone to heaven to dwell.

G.W. Louise [*sic*], New Braunfels, 1874-1893.

METAL grave marker with poetic epitaph for Lucia Scheel, 1891-1901, Honey Creek Cemetery, Comal County, 1901. For text of epitaph see No. 6.

—*Photo, T.G.J., 1978.*

3.

Ich war der Mutter Trost,
Dem Vater eine Freude,
Gott aber liebt' mich mehr,
Denn diese alle beide.
Kaum blüht' ich auf,
Da fiel ich ab,
Fiel aus der Wiege in das Grab.
Otto H.F. Holz, New Braunfels, 1882-1884.

My mother's consolation,
My father's greatest love,
But God loved me more,
Took me to Himself above.
I had hardly blossomed out,
When I fell down,
Fell from the cradle into the tomb.

4.

Es war ein unschuldig's Kindlein,
Dieses Friedhofs Grundstein.
Mathilda Laubach, Honey Creek, Comal Co., 1889. (Copied by T.G.J.)

This innocent child, so dear,
Was the first one buried here.

5.

Komm, Schäflein mein,
Bei mir sollst sein.
Agatha Syring, Honey Creek, Comal Co., 1903-1903.

Come, my little lamb,
And be where I am.

6.

Here is one of the most unusual epitaphs in the Texas German Belt, and it seems to be indigenous to Texas.

Des Morgens Schlangenbiss
Macht abends dir den Himmel g'wiss
(gewiss).
Lucia Scheel, Honey Creek Cemetery, Comal Co., 1891-1901. (Copied by T.G.J.)

A morning bite by a snake
By evening brought heaven in its wake.

7.

Sein Leben war ein Augenblick,
Ein Frühlingstraum, sein Erdenglück.
Albert Monken, Boerne, 1898-1899.

His life was but a moment's play;
A dream in spring, his earthly stay.

8.

Das Mägdlein schläft,
Gönnt ihm die süsse Ruh'.
Durch Blumen blickt sein friedvoll Gesicht
Und spricht:
"Ihr trauernd Lieben
Mein verzaget nicht."
Elise Fellbaum, Comfort, 1874-1889.

The maiden sleeps,
Grant her the sweet repose.
Through blossoms now her face, so peaceful, keeps
And speaks to those
Who mourn: "Despair
not in your woes."

9.

This stone has the usual Catholic cross on top, carved flowers, and a lamb.

Dieses kleinen Hügels dunkler Schatten

The dark shadow of this mound

Deckt das Liebste zweier Ehegatten. Hides the dearest the parents had found.

Ihres teuren Kindes ird'sche Hülle The earthly remains of their precious child

Modert in des Grabes Stille. Are lying in the quiet ground.
Ruhe gut, Helene, ruh' in Frieden, Sleep well, Helene, and rest in peace,
Jenseits ist ein Wiederseh'n beschieden. Up yonder we will find release.

Helene Eberle, St. Mary's Cemetery, Fredericksburg, 1884-1885. (Copied by A.E.)

10.

Ruhe sanft in Gottes Schoss, Gently rest in the bosom of God.
Seligkeit sei dir zum Loos. May blessedness now be your lot.
Einst beim frohen Auferstehn Some day when we arise again,
Werden wir uns wiedersehn. Then we will all meet again.

Gustav, *Söhnlein* (little son) of Gustav and Maria Bohmert. Rosehill Cemetery, near Tom Ball, Harris Co., 1894-1895.

EPITAPHS FOR ADULTS

11.

Du gingst dem Tode froh entgegen, You gladly faced death's cold caressing;

Zum Himmel war dein letzter Blick; To heaven, above, your final gaze;
Dort lohnet dich des Vaters Segen, There God, the Father, gives his blessing,

Dort blühet dir das ewige Leben. Eternal joy for endless days.

Julius Voigt, New Braunfels, 1901. Also August Weiss, Pflugerville, 1917. Also Carl Krause, 1937, Louise Krause, Brenham, 1931.

12.

Du warst so fromm, voll Liebe, treu bescheiden, You were so pious, loving, modest, true;
Mit dir entflohen unsere Freuden Our joys all went away with you.

Anna Weil, *geb.* Koehler, New Braunfels, 1894. Also Emma Dietert Randow, Zorn, Guadalupe Co., 1909. Also Bertina Herbst, Comfort, 1918. Also Martha Karger Herbst and others, Comfort.

13.

Wir sehen uns in bessern Welten,
Denn zu gut warst du für diese hier;

Wo der Himmelvater wird vergelten
Mutterlieb und Vaterstreue dir.
Katharine Simon, New Braunfels, 1892.

We'll see each other in better days,
You were too good for this world here,
Where God in heaven for you repays
The love of Father and Mother, dear.

14.

Das Irdische mag in Staub vergehn,
Für Geister gibt's ein Wiedersehn.
J. Peter Magnus, New Braunfels, 1886.

Our earthly bodies will return to dust,
But spirits have eternal trust.

15.

Teurer Gatte, liebe Kinder,
Die ihr schmerzlich mich beweint,
Hofft der Todesüberwinder
Selig wieder uns vereint.
Ulricke Voigt, *geb.* Trebs, New Braunfels, 1883.

Faithful husband, loving children,
You who weep in pain for me,
Hope the conquerer of the grave
will unite us eternally.

16.

Lebt wohl, ihr Lieben, klagt nicht mehr!
Ich musst' euch lassen einsam.
Hier sanft schlummre ich im Schattenland,
Bis uns vereint ein ewig Land.
Joh. Heinrich Schulte, New Braunfels, 1800's.

Farewell, belovéd, weep no more;

I left you on a lonely shore;
And here in shadow land I lie

Until we meet in the bye and bye.

17.

Christus wischte ab Euch alle Thränen.
Ihr habt schon, wonach wir uns erst sehnen.
Euch ist gesungen,

Was durch keines Ohr allhier gedrungen.,
New Braunfel, the 1800's

Christ has dried all tears for you.
You attained what we seek too.

For you, was sung th' eternal word,

Like never human ear has heard.

18.

Zu frueh schlug diese bittre Stunde,
Die Dich aus unsrer Mitte nahm,
Doch troestend toent aus unsrem Munde:
"Was Gott thut, das ist wohlgetan."

Dies Wort stillt unser banges Flehen.
Ach ruhe sanft, auf Wiedersehen.
Olga Glenewinkel, Zorn Cemetery, Guadalupe County, 1925. (Copied by R.H.)

Your bitter hour struck too early
And took you from our midst away,
But our voices say it fairly:

"What God does that's well done today."

These words relieve our anxious pain;
Rest in peace, auf Wiederseh'n."

19.

Er schied hinueber in das ewige Licht;
Sein Wirken bleibt in Erinnerung, schwindet nicht.
Oskar Erich Dietert, Zorn Cemetery, Guadalupe County, 1918. (Copied by R.H.)

He went away to eternal light;
His work endures, his memory's bright.

20.

Von dem Frommen ist das eigen,
Wenn seine Todes Kaempfe zeigen,
Dass er sterbend froehlich spricht,
Mein Gewissen quaelt mich nicht.
Maria Trapp, *geb,* Glenewinkel, Zorn Cemetery, Guadalupe County, 1912. (Copied by R.H.)

Of a pious one this is a sign,
That in his pangs of death he'll pine
And speak so joyfully and free,
My conscience does not trouble me.

21.

So schlummre sanft, Du gute Mutter,
Das Grab entriss Dich uns zu früh.
Du warst uns Schutz, Du warst Berater,
Ach wir vergessen deiner nie.
Ida Bartels, Smithson Valley, Comal County, 1908.

Now gently sleep, good Mother, dear.
The grave took you from us too soon.
You were our guardian, our counsel, you,
And oh, we'll not forget you here.

22.

Schlaf süss in kalter Erde,
Nichts störe deine Ruh',
Und Rasen grün und duftend
Deck' deine Asche zu.
Joachim Pantermühl, Twin Sisters, Blanco County, 1876.

Sweetly sleep in the cold earth,
May none disturb your rest,
And green and fragrant grasses
May cover up your ashes.

23.

Hier muss alles schwinden,
Dort werden wir uns wiederfinden.
Elise F. Uecker, Honey Creek, Comal County, 1930.

All must pass away down here;
Up there we'll meet again, don't fear.

24.

Thränen, fliesset, rinnet
Wohl um den Edlen hier!
Blumen, spriesset blühet
Zu des Todten Ehr!
Carl Adam, Boerne, 1879.

Let tears of sorrow flow
For this our noble friend;
Let flowers bloom and grow
And honor to him lend.

25.

On the memorial monument by the mass grave of the thirty-five men who lost their lives in the Battle of the Nueces and on the Rio Grande while they were on their way to join the Union forces during the Civil War, 1862, stands the following inscription:

Treue der Union.
Comfort.

Men loyal to the Union.

26.

Im Lande, wo's kein Scheiden giebt,
Vereint [Vereinet] Gott, die sich geliebt.
Fritz Nickel, Comfort, 1919. Also M.A. Gollnick, Denton County, 1917 (T.G.J.) And August Kaus, Cypress Mills, Blanco County, 1939.

In the land of no parting, above,
God unites those who here shared love.

27.

Er schlief hinüber in das ewige Licht,
Sein Wirken bleibt, Erinnerung schwindet nicht.
Robert Schladoer, Comfort, 1919. Also Johann Blümel, Comfort, 1898, but his one has *schlummert* (slumbers) instead of *schwindet* (disappears).

He went up yonder to eternal light;
His work remains, remembrance still is bright.

28.

Sinkt der Leib hinab zum Staube,
Führt zum Schauen uns der Glaube.
Josephine Bluemel, Comfort, 1914.

When our bodies turn to dust,
Faith leads us on to sight and trust.

GRAVE marker with rhymed epitaph for Mrs. Ella Schild, nee Lich, in the Comfort Cemetery, 1920. For text see Epitaph No. 30.
—*Photo, T.G.J., 1979.*

29.

The following epitaph is unusual inasmuch as it alludes to the man's vocation, farming.

Hier nun ruhet,	Here rests the one
der die Erde sechzig	Who plowed the soil
Jahre gepflüget.	Through sixty years of toil.

Ferdinand Schulze, Comfort, 1900.

30.

Du Theure hast nun ausgelitten	Belovéd, you suffered to the end,
Und sinkst zu früh ins stille Grab.	You fell too early into the grave.
Der Schöpfer liess sich nicht erbitten,	Your creator could not be moved;
Der dir ein bessres Leben gab.	To you a better life He gave.

Mrs. Ella Schild, nee Lich, Comfort, 1920.

31.

In this epitaph there is something of the immigrant's feeling of loneliness over death far from his native homeland.

Ich starb hier im fremden Land
Doch ich ruh in Gotteshand
Wie in meinem Vaterland.
John Lamon, Castroville, 1882.

I died here in a foreign land,
And yet I rest in God's own hand,
As I would rest in my fatherland.

32.

Unser Geist ist hoch erhoben,
Auf wiedersehn dort droben.

Our spirits now on high are raised
Till we meet again, and God be praised.

Jacob Bendelle, Castroville, 1910.

33.

Hier schloss sich der Verklärten Blick,
So war es, höchster Gott, dein Wille,
Hier nahm die Erde ihre Hülle,
Der Himmel ihren Geist zurück.
M. Anna Rohrbach, Castroville, 1890.

Here the transfigured closed her eyes,
Thus, highest God, it was your will,
Here where the earth received her hull,
And to heaven, above, her spirit flies.

34.

Gattin aus dem Arm des Gatten,
Eltern aus der Kindercreis [...Kinder Kreis,]
Deckt des Todes stiller Schatten,
Er umfängt Kind, Jüngling, Greis.
Katharine Nay, St. Dominic Cemetery, Old D'Hanis, Medina County, 1869.

Wife from husband's empty arms,
Parents from their children flung,

Death's still shadow spreads its harms,
It surrounds the old, the young.

35.

The following is one of the oldest epitaphs in the present collection. Some words are illegible and I reconstructed them as shown in brackets. Note the six-line rhyme, including one dialectal or archaic word, *Genicht*.

Horcht, was der todte Vater spricht,
Ihr hinterlassene weinet nicht,
Seid treu dem Glauben u. [der] Pflicht.
Tragt [euer Kreuz] der Leidenschaft Genicht [geneigt],

Listen to your dead father speak:
You mourners, do not cry and weep.
Be loyal to your faith and duty,
Bear your cross of sorrow, deep,

69

THE author copying an epitaph from a tombstone in St. Dominic Cemetery, Old D'Hanis, Medina Co.

—*Photo by T.G.J., 1979.*

Und tretet, wenn das Herz [ein] bricht,	And when your hearts from sorrow break,
Mit Freuden vor des Herrn Gericht.	With joy before God's judgment wake.

Jos. Zurcher, St. Dominic Cemetery, Old D'Hanis, Medina County, 1860.

36.

Die gerechten Seelen	The righteous souls
Sind in Gottes Hand	Are in God's hand
In des Friedens ew'ger	In the peace of the eternal
Faterland. [sic.]	Fatherland.

Charlie Heckel, Rocky Cemetery, Blanco County, 1917.

37.

Ach zu früh bist du geschieden,
Und umsonst war unser Flehn,
Ruhe nun in Gottes Frieden,
Bis wir einst uns wiedersehn.
Philip Nocker, St. Joseph's Cemetery, San Antonio, 1882.

Oh, you left us all too soon,
And our pleas were all in vain;
Gently rest in the peace of God
Until we meet each other again.

38.

Im Grab ist Ruh,
Auf Erden Schmerz.
Dann schlummre sanft,
Du gutes Herz.
Wilhelm Winkler, St. Joseph's Cemetery, San Antonio, 1909.

In the grave is rest,
On earth is fear (Lit., pain)
So slumber gently,
Good Heart, so dear.

39.

Der ernste Todesengel senkt
Die Fackel, eh der Mensch es denkt,

Er nimmt ihm seine Leiden ab
Und legt ihn sanft ins stille Grab.
Friedrich Miesner, Brenham, 1865.

The solemn angel of death will sink
And lower the torch ere man can think;
He takes his suff'rings all away
And puts him in his grave today.

40.

Wie früh brach deine Knospe ab,
Wie früh sankst du ins kühle Grab.
Du warst uns lieb in diesem Leben,
Drum sei dies Denkmal dir gegeben.
Julius F. Wilhelm, Brenham, 1889.

Your bud of life broke off too soon;
You sank into the grave by noon.
You were so dear to us alone,
So we have placed for you this stone.

41.

Wie ein sanfter Schlummer, der die Müden
Nach der Tagesarbeit überfällt,
So des Frommen Tod; er schläft in Frieden
Sanft hinüber in die bessere Welt.
Johannes Giese, Sr., Bethlehem Lutheran Cemetery, Round Top, 1901. (Copied by T.G.J.)

Like a gentle slumber which befalls

The weary after days of toil and grace,
So is the death of a pious man; he sleeps
In peace and goes up to a better place.

42.

O Friede, Friede ihm die Engel winken!
Zum Lande [hin] auf, wo seine Palme blüht;
Ins finstre Grab musst' seine Hülle sinken,
Weil hell dem Geiste dort das Leben glüht.
Alfred Pochmann, Bethlehem Lutheran Cemetery, Round Top, 1898. (Copied by T.G.J.)

Oh peace, oh peace for him the angels beckon
Up to the land wherein his palm tree grows.
Into the gloomy grave his body fell,
But in the life above his spirit glows.

43.

Die Ruhe folgt nach langen Kummertagen,
Wenn Staub von unsrer Seele sinkt,
Wir wollen nicht den Schlafenden beklagen,
Dem jetzt ein ewig lichter Morgen winkt.
Serbin, Lee County, 1908. Also Johann & Marie Schulze, Twin Sisters, 1888 and 1893. (Copied by T.G.J.)

His rest comes after many a painful day,
When the dust from our spirits falls.
We'll not bemoan the sleeper while a ray

Of everlasting morning calls.

44.

Traurig blicken wir dir nach
In dein stilles Schlafgemach,
Glauben an ein Auferstehn,
Freuen uns auf's Wiedersehn
Anton Golly, Meyersville, 1884. (Copied by T.G.J.)

In sadness we must see you go
To your still abode of woe,
But our faith o'ercomes our pain,
And we'll rejoice in meeting again.

45.

Darum, ihr Eitelkeiten!
Lust, Weisheit, Schütze, Pracht!
Ihr Freunde meiner Zeiten!
Ihr Freunde, gute Nacht!
Und gute Nacht, ihr Glieder!
Schlaft wohl in stiller Gruft.
Wir sehn uns freudig wieder,
Wenn Gottes Stimm' uns ruft.
Joh. Kilian, Serbin, 1884. (Copied by T.G.J.)

Therefore, you vanities:
Joy, wisdom, shelter, pride,
You friends of former days,
You friends, I'll say Good Night.
I'll say Good Night, my body.
Sleep well in the silent grave.
We'll happily meet again
When God calls us to save.

46.

Nach Todesschmerz und Grabesruh
Führt Christus uns dem Himmel zu.
Louise M. Presler, Salem Lutheran Cemetery, near Tom Ball, Harris County, 1922.

From pangs of death and peaceful rest
Christ leads to heaven to be blest.

47.

Christi Blut und Gerechtigkeit,
Das ist mein Schmuck und Ehrenkleid:
Damit will ich vor Gott bestehn,
Wenn ich zum Himmel werd' eingehn.
Julius H. Juergen, Rose Hill Cemetery, near Tom Ball, Harris County, 1934.

Christ's blood and righteousness,
These are my jewels and honored dress;
With these before my God I'll stand
When I will enter the heavenly land.

48.

The following epitaph is the oldest in the present collection.

O, lieber Freund, gedenke mein,
In dein Gebet mich schlüsse [schliesse] ein.
Lebe stets als frommer Christ,
Der seine Pflichten nicht vergisst.
Bereite dich zu jeder Zeit
Und sorge für die Ewigkeit.
Frelsburg Catholic Cemetery, Colorado County, 1856.

Oh, dear friend, I want to be
Remembered in a prayer by thee.
Live always as a Christian, dear,
Who ne'er forgets his duty here,
Be ready at all times and be
Concerned about eternity.

49.

Gottlob! so ist's gekommen,
Er hat mich aufgenommen
In sein verklärtes Reich.
In Jesu Gnadengaben
Darf ich mein Geist nun laben,
O sein Erbarmen ist so gross!
Henrietta Plattow, Pflugerville, Travis County, 1889.

Praise God! My time has come;
He took me to His home,
To His transfigured realm.
By Jesus' gifts of grace
My soul may take its place;
His mercy will o'erwhelm.

50.

Verbirg dein liebes Angesicht
Im kühlen Erdenschoss.
Wer hier gelebt in Christi Licht,
Der erbt ein selig Loos.
Emma G.L. Pfluger, Pflugerville, 1886.

Now hide your precious face
In the earth's womb and wait;
Who's lived by Christian grace
Will gain a blissful fate.

> O lieber Freund gedenke mein
> In dein Gebet mich schlüsse ein.
> Lebe stets als frommer Christ
> Der seine Pflichten nicht vergist.
> Bereite dich zu jeder zeit
> Und sorge für die Ewigkeit

POETIC epitaph engraved in the old German lettering, Frelsburg Catholic Cemetery, Colorado Co., 1856. Retouched rubbing by T.G.J., 1980. For text see Epitaph No. 48.

51.

Aus dem Staub der morschen Hülle
Schwebt der Geist zu Gott empor.
Friedrich Lochte, Fredericksburg, 1867.

From the crumbling mortal frame
Will our God the spirit claim.

52.

Wir haben herzlich dich geliebt,
Dein Tod nun innig uns betrübt,

Und ach wir können's nicht verstehn,
Dass du so bald sollst von uns gehn.

Wilhelm Feller, Fredericksburg, 1864.

We loved you much and dearly,
Your death now makes us sad sincerely.

And oh, we cannot understand
That you should leave our happy land.

53.

Ach zu früh bist du geschieden
Doch Gottes Wille muss gescheh'n.
Nun ruhe sanft in Frieden,
Bis dass wir uns einst wiederseh'n.
Christine, *Tochter des* Friedrich & Mathilda Grobe, Fredericksburg, 1888.

All too early you went away,
But God's will must be done today.
Rest in peace within God's love,
Until we meet again above.

54.

Als Gatte, als Vater, als Freund
Ruht hier, von vielen beweint,
Ein Mann, der Tugend stets übte
Und Treue und Redlichkeit liebte.

Max H. Reinbach, St. Mary's Cemetery, Fredericksburg, 1896.

As husband, as father, as friend,
By many bemoaned at his end,
Here rests a virtuous soul,
Loyalty and honesty were his goal.

55.

O Mutter, demutsvoll und rein,

Schliesz [sic.] in dein Liebe volles [sic.] Herz uns ein.

Therese Moritz, nee Kopp, St. Mary's Cemetery, Fredericksburg, 1894.

Oh Mother, humble, meek, and pure,
Keep us in your heart secure.

56.

Kämpfer aus der Leidensnacht,
Bist du nun zum Licht erwacht;

Lebe in dem ewigen Frieden,
Für den du gewirkt hienieden.

Pastor Christian Koch, Fredericksburg, 1886.

Soldier from the night of sorrow,
You awoke to the light of the morrow.

May you live in eternal peace
For which you worked without surcease.

57.

Einst ist seliges Entzücken,
Unsre Sehnsucht ist gestillt,
Friede wird uns dort beglücken,
Wo was wir gehofft erfüllt.

Heinrich Jordan, Fredericksburg, 1879.

Some day blissful joy and rapture
And our yearning all are stilled.
Peace will hold us and will capture,
What we hoped for is fulfilled.

58.

The following terse epitaph in prose tells the story in three words:

Ermordet von Indianern.

Heinrich Grobe, Fredericksburg, 1862.

Murdered by Indians.

59.

Nach überstand'nen schweren Leiden
Bin ich versetzt in hohen Freuden.

Johann Melchoir Bauer, Bauer Cemetery, Mason County, 1874. (Copied by F.D.B.)

After suff'ring I have overcome
To get great joys in my future home.

60.

Schnell muss alles Schöne schwinden	Quickly will all beauty fade
In des Lebens Blüthenzeit.	In our youthful blossom time.
Herrlich wirst du es finden	You will find it all repaid
In dem Land der Ewigkeit.	In eternity, subline.

Franziska Bauer, *geb'ne* Gatt, Bauer Cemetery, Mason County, 1897. (Copied by F.D.B.)

61.

Ruhe sanft, du edles Herz,	Rest gently, you noble heart,
In Jesu ruhe aus,	Rest well in Jesus' arms,
Dich rief er von der Erde Schmerz.	He called you from your earthly part.

Gustave Topf, Lindsay, 1894.

62.

The following inscriptions are a combined epitaph for a married couple in the Lindsay, Cooke County, Catholic Cemetery. There is a common stone, but the "Jesus" epitaph for the "Father" and the "Mary" verse for the "Mother" are separate.

Süsses Herz,	Dear heart,
Jesus sei meine Liebe	May Jesus be my love.

    F.J. Rohenkohl, "Father," 1897.

Süsses Herz,	Dear heart,
Maria sei meine Rettung.	May Mary be my salvation.

    K. Rohenkohl, "Mother," 1918.

63.

Was die Mutter uns gewesen,	What our mother meant to all
Kann man nicht am Grabstein lesen.	Can't be read on tombstones, tall;
Eingegraben wie im Erz	It's engraved and will ever stay
Ist es in der Kinder Herz.	In her children's hearts today.
Gott, der Herr der Welten,	God, the Lord of all the world,
Soll's ihr tausendfach vergelten.	Will repay a thousandfold.

Theresia Bockholt, Catholic Cemetery, Westphalia, Falls County, 1941. (Copied by T.G.J.)

The poetic epitaphs printed above were taken mostly from the Texas German Belt, but there are also a few from far North Texas. These inscriptions range from two lines to six, but the majority are four lines in length. There are also longer poems, but not many, and these were not included in the collection. Two prose inscriptions, numbers 25 and 58, are included because of their uniqueness.

8.

TRADITIONAL AND FAMILIAR SONGS.

The German immigrants in Texas have always been great singers. In the 1850's they began to organize singers' clubs, and in the course of the years singing societies were formed in almost all the German settlements. Many of these clubs had interesting names, like the *Frohsinn* (Good Cheer) group of Dallas, the *Liederkranz* (Choral Society), the *Sängerbund* (Choral Club), and the *Damenchor* (Ladies Chorus) of Houston, the *Sängerrunde* (Singing Circle) of Austin, and the *Beethoven Männerchor* (Men's Chorus), the *Teutonia*, and the *Mendelssohn* clubs of San Antonio. New Braunfels had, at various times, five different clubs with such names as *Germania, Echo, Concordia*, and *Liedertafel* (glee club). Galveston had a *Salamander* club, Sattler had its *Walhalla* group, Grapetown had its *Eintracht* (Concordia or harmony) singers, and Fredericksburg had an *Arion Männerchor* (Arion men's chorus). There were literally dozens of these clubs, and many have survived to the present day.

The clubs were organized into several state singers leagues, and annual song festivals *(Sängerfeste)* were held, where the various clubs vied with each other in singing their songs. Two of these leagues have survived to the present day: The *Deutsch-Texanischer Sängerbund* (the German-Texas State Singers' League) and the *Gebirgssängerbund* (Hill Country Singers' League), and their song festivals are held annually to the present day.

These singing societies have been the chief preservers of the German-Texas song traditions, but also some non-members and school teachers and children kept up an interest in the old songs. The glee clubs have various song books of their own from which they sing their concerts *a cappela,* but the members and their friends also sing informally from memory on various occasions.

Not too many of the songs used by the singing societies are to be found in the present collection because they are available in the song books of the clubs. Nevertheless, some are included along with other

INVITATION to a "Sing Along" in New Braunfels, Texas: "Welcome, and enjoy a jolly good time."

German songs. For the purpose of the present collection, the songs are placed in two related groups and printed in two separate chapters: (1) familiar and traditional songs, and (2) drinking songs. The present chapter deals with some of traditional songs, not only *Sängerbund* (Singers' League) items, but also generally known songs that are still popular in the former German-speaking communities. They are also sung by students in German classes throughout the country. The words and the musical notes can be found in most German song books and the songs can be heard on records and tapes.

What is new in the present collection are the author-collector's original, singable English translations. It is hoped that the new renditions of these universally liked songs will help preserve them for posterity, even after the people's knowledge of German may gradually fade away. And then, too, the translations will make the words available to English-speaking people. These songs, as much as anything else, are a vital part of the German-Texas lore and heritage.

Some of these songs might be considered folk songs but others were written by well known poets and composers. They were sung everywhere in Germany in the nineteenth century and were brought to Texas by the German immigrants; and here they may have survived better than in Germany itself. The nostalgic flavor of the songs and their expression of yearning for the old country appealed to these people who were far removed from their former homeland. Moreover, the settlers who came to Texas had been brought up on German romanticism and on sentimental songs of love and friendship. The transplanted German people treasured this tradition in Texas as they had in their native lands, perhaps even more so because the songs were a strong link that tied them closely to their distant friends and homes.

HERZLICHST GRUESSEN

BEETHOVEN MAENNERCHOR
BEETHOVEN DAMENCHOR
BEETHOVEN BAND

BEETHOVEN HEIM

422 Pereida St.

San Antonio, Texas

BEETHOVEN MAENNERCHOR

SAN ANTONIO, TEXAS

Gegruendet: 23. Februar 1867

Ehren-Praesident	Henry Riemer
	Dr. Alex L. Rehag
Praesident	Lee H. Gastinger
Vize-Praesident	Joe Rabke
Sekretaer-Schatzmeister	George M. Pankratz
Dirigent	Otto E. Ransleben
Pianistin	Frau Marguerite Dexter

GREETINGS from the two Beethoven Choirs and the Band of San Antonio, Texas.

—*Courtesy, Institute of Texan Cultures.*

1.

Freut euch des Lebens,
Freut euch des Lebens,
Weil noch das Lämpchen glüht,
Pflücket die Rose, eh' sie verblüht.

Man schafft so gern sich Sorg' und Müh',
Sucht Dornen auf und findet sie

Und lässt das Veilchen unbemerkt,
Das dort am Wege blüht.
Freut euch des Lebens,
Eh' es verblüht.

(G.J.J.—See Schmidt, 107, for additional stanzas.)

Naegli, 1793.

Relish life's pleasures
While still the lamplight's bright,
Pluck ever the roses ere covered with blight,

We like to make much care and work,

Seek out the thorns where'er they lurk,

And leave the violets unseen
That by the pathway bloom.
Relish life's pleasures
While they still bloom.

2.

Du, du liegst mir im Herzen,
Du, du liegst mir im Sinn;
Du, du machst mir viel Schmerzen,
Weisst nicht, wie gut ich dir bin.
Ja, ja, ja, ja,
Weisst nicht, wie gut ich dir bin.

So, so wie ich dich liebe,
So, so liebe auch mich!
Die, die zärtlichsten Triebe
Fühle ich einzig für dich.
Ja, ja, ja, ja,
Fühle ich einzig für dich.

Doch, doch, darf ich dir trauen,
Dir, dir mit leichtem Sinn?
Du, du kannst auf mich bauen,
Weisst ja wie gut ich dir bin.
Ja, ja, ja, ja,
Weisst ja, wie gut ich dir bin.

Und, und wenn in der Ferne
Mir, mir dein Bild erscheint,
Dann, dann wünscht' ich so gerne,
Dass uns die Liebe vereint.
Ja, ja, ja, ja,
Dass uns die Liebe vereint.
Volkslied (Folksong) (G.J.J. & C.E.S.—See Alexis, 188.)

You, you are in my heart, dear,
You, you are in my mind;
You, you make me much heartache,
Don't know how much I love you.
Yes, yes, yes, yes,
Don't know how much I love you.

How, how, how much I love you,
So, so, so love me too.
The, the tenderest feelings,
These I have only for you.
Yes, yes, yes, yes,
These I have only for you.

But, but can I still trust you,
You, you with fickle mind?
You, you can ever trust me,
Knowing how much I love you.
Yes, yes, yes, yes,
Knowing how much I love you.

And, and when in far places
Your, your image appears,
Then, then wish I so strongly
That love us ever unite.
Yes, yes, yes, yes,
Love us forever unite.

3.

Horch, was kommt von draussen rein,	Hark, who's coming, walking by,
Hollahi, hollaho.	Hollahi, hollaho!
Wird wohl mein Feinsliebchen sein.	That must be my sweetie pie,
Hollahiaho!	Hollahiaho!
Geht vorbei und schaut nicht rein.	Won't come in, oh why, oh why?
Hollahi, hollaho,	Hollahi, hollaho!
Wird's wohl nicht gewesen sein.	Can't have been my sweetie pie.
Hollahiaho!	Hollahiaho!
Leute haben's oft gesagt,	People saw him [her] walking by,
Hollahi, hollaho!	Hollahi, hollaho!
Dass ich ein Feinsliebchen hab'.	Said I had a sweetie pie,
Hollahiaho!	Hollahiaho!
Lass sie reden, ich schweig still,	Let them gossip; I'll keep still,
Hollahi, hollaho,	Hollahi, hollaho.
Kann ja lieben, wen ich will,	I can love whome'er I will,
Hollahiaho!	Hollahiaho!
Wenn ich einst gestorben bin,	And some day when I have died,
Hollahi, hollaho!	Hollahi, hollaho!
Trägt man mich zum Friedhof hin.	They will bury me by his [her] side,
Hollahiaho!	Hollahiaho!
Setzt man mir einen Leichenstein,	On the stone they'll write a lot,
Hollahi, hollaho!	Hollahi, hollaho!
Schreibt darauf "Vergiss nicht mein."	And they'll say: Forget-me-not,"
Hollahiaho!	Hollahiaho!
(M.M.J. & T.K.)	

4.

Das zerbrochene Ringlein.

In einem kühlen Grunde
Da geht ein Mühlenrad,
Mein' Liebste ist verschwunden,
Die dort gewohnet hat.
(Repeat last 2 lines)

Sie hat mir treu versprochen,
Gab mir ein'n Ring dabei,
Sie hat die Treu gebrochen,
Mein Ringlein sprang entzwei.
(Repeat)

Ich möcht' als Spielmann reisen
Weit in die Welt hinaus
Und singen meine Weisen
Und gehn von Haus zu Haus.
(Repeat)

Ich möcht' als Reiter fliegen
Wohl in die blut'ge Schlacht,
Um stille Feuer liegen
Im Feld bei dunkler Nacht.
(Repeat)

Hör' ich das Mühlrad gehen:
Ich weiss nicht, was ich will—
Ich möcht' am liebsten sterben,
Da wär's auf einmal still!
(Repeat)

Joseph von Eichendorff, 1809. Fredrich Glück, 1814. (C.E.S. & G.J.J.—Alexis, 189.)

The Broken Ring

Down in cool river bottoms
There goes a millwheel round;
My sweetheart there has vanished
Who heard the groaning sound.
(Repeat last 2 lines)

She promised to be faithful,
Gave me a ring, so true;
But, oh, she wasn't loyal;
My ring then broke in two.
(Repeat)

Like a minstrel I would wander,
Far away I'd like to roam,
And sing my songs in sadness
And go from home to home.
(Repeat)

Like a horseman I'd go riding
Far to the bloody fight,
And lie by quiet campfires
In the battlefield at night.
(Repeat)

I hear the millwheel turning;
I don't known what is best;
I'd like to leave and perish,
Then all would be at rest.
(Repeat)

Ach, wie ist's möglich dann,
Dass ich dich lassen kann?
Hab' dich von Herzen lieb,
Das glaube mir!
Du hast die Seele mein
So ganz genommen ein,
Dass ich kein' andre lieb,
Als dich allein.

Blau ist ein Blümelein,
Das heisst Vergissnichtmein:
Dies Blümlein leg ans Herz
Und denk an mich!
Stirbt Blüt' und Hoffnung gleich,
Wir sind an Liebe reich
Denn die stirbt nie bei mir!
Das glaube mir!

Wär' ich ein Vögelein,
Wollt' ich bald bei dir sein,
Scheut' Falk' und Habicht nicht,
Flög ich zu dir.
Schöss' mich ein Jäger tot,
Fiel ich in deinen Schoss,
Säh'st du mich traurig an
Gern stürb' ich dann.

(*Volkslied,* Folksong. G.J.J. & C.E.S.—See Bacon, *Vorwärts,* 124-125.)

Oh, how is it possible then
That I can leave you when
With all my heart I love;
This do believe.
You have this soul of mine
So fully taken in
That no one else I love
But you alone.

Blue is a flowerlet
That's called Forget-me-not;
Place it upon your heart
And think of me.
Though flower and hope may die,
We are so rich in love,
And it will never die,
This do believe.

Were I a little bird,
I would be with you soon;
I'd fear no falcon's claws
And fly to you,
If hunters shot me dead,
I'd fall into your lap;
If then your heart were sad,
Gladly I'd die.

6.

Muss i denn, muss i denn	Must I then, must I then
Zum Städtele hinaus, Städtele hinaus,	From my town go away, town go away,
Und du, mei Schatz, bleibst hier?	And you, my love, stay here?
Wenn i komm, wenn i komm,	When I come, when I come,
Wenn i wiederum komm, wiederum komm,	When I come back again, come back again,
Kehr i ein, mei Schatz, bei dir.	I will come to you, my dear.
Kann i gleich nit allweil bei dir sein,	Though I can't be with you all the time,
Han i doch mei Freud an dir.	I still love you, my dear.
Wenn i komm, wenn i komm,	When I come, when I come,
Wenn i wiederum komm, wiederum komm,	When I come back again, come back again,
Kehr i ein, mei Schatz, bei dir.	I will come to you, my dear.
Wie du weinst, wie du weinst,	How you cry, how you cry
Dass i wandere muss, wandere muss,	That I must go away, must go away,
Wie, wenn d'Lieb' jetzt wär vorbei!	As though our love were past,
Sind au drauss, sind au drauss	In the world, in the world
Der Mädele viel, Mädele viel,	Many gals may be, gals may be,
Lieber Schatz, i bleib dir treu.	Dear heart, I will stay true.
Denk du nit, wenn i ein andre seh,	Don't think when other girls I see
So sei mei Lieb vorbei.	That our love will go away.
Sind au drauss, sind au drauss	In the world, in the world
Der Mädele viel, Mädele viel,	Many gals may be, gals may be,
Lieber Schatz, i bleib dir treu.	Dear heart, I will stay true.

(E.W.J. & G.J.J.—See Schmidt, 88.)

7.

Der Lindenbaum.

Am Brunnen vor dem Tore,
Da steht ein Lindenbaum;
Ich träumt' in seinem Schatten
So manchen süssen Traum.
Ich schnitt in seine Rinde
So manches liebe Wort;
Es zog in Freud' und Leide
Zu ihm mich immer fort.
(Repeat line)

Ich musst' auch heute wandern
Vorbei in tiefer Nacht,
Da hab' ich noch im Dunkel
Die Augen zugemacht.
Und seine Zweige rauschten,
Als riefen sie mir zu:
Komm her zu mir, Geselle,
Hier find'st du deine Ruh!
(Repeat)

Die kalten Winde bliessen
Mir grad ins Angesicht,
Der Hut flog mir vom Kopfe,
Ich wendete mich nicht.
Nun bin ich manche Stunde
Entfernt von jenem Ort,
Und immer hör' ich's rauschen:
Du fändest Ruhe dort.
(Repeat)

Wilhelm Müller, Franz Schubert (C.E.S. & G.J.J.—See Alexis, 180.)

The Linden Tree.

By the fountain near the portals
There stands a linden tree,
I dreamed beneath its shadow
So many a dream of thee.
I cut into its bark there
So many a word of love;
It called me back in sorrow
And joy from up above.
(Repeat)

Today I had to wander
Along in deepest night;
I closed in night-time darkness
My eyes from any sight.
And there its twigs were rustling
As though they called to me:
Come here to me, my fellow,
Here's rest and peace for thee.
(Repeat)

The icy winds were blowing,
Right in my face they blew,
My hat flew from my head then,
I knew not where it flew.
Now I am many hours
Away from yonder tree,
And always hear the rustling:
Here peace would be for thee.
(Repeat)

8.

Many of the German settlers in Texas were, and still are, fond of hunting, like Bishop Hubertus of ancient times, whose name I heard mentioned by one of my informants in Sisterdale. *Schützenvereine* (Rifle Clubs) were organized and *Schützenfeste* (Rifle festivals) were held. Like the singing clubs, some of the rifle clubs have survived to the present day, and the people still sing their hunting songs. Here is one of the best loved songs of this kind, the *Jägerlied* (Hunter's Song):

Im Wald und auf der Heide	In woods and on the meadows,
Da such' ich meine Freude,	I seek my joy and pleasures,
Ich bin ein Jägersmann,	I am a hunting man.
(Repeat line)	(Repeat line)
Die Forsten treu zu pflegen,	I tend the forest truly,
Das Wildpret zu erlegen,	I shoot the game, and surely
Mein' Lust hab' ich daran.	This is my joy and fun.
(Repeat line)	(Repeat line)
Halli, hallo, halli, hallo,	Halli, hallo, halli, hallo,
Mein' Lust hab ich daran	This is my joy and fun.
Trag' ich in meiner Tasche	And in my pouch I carry
Ein Trünklein in der Flasche,	A little flask of spirits,
Zwei Bisschen liebes Brot;	Some bits of precious bread;
(Repeat line)	(Repeat line)
Brennt lustig meine Pfeife,	And while my pipe is burning,
Wenn ich den Forst durchstreife,	I'll cross the forest roaming,
Da hat es keine Not.	There's nothing else I need.
(Repeat line)	(Repeat line)
Halli, hallo, halli, hallo,	Halli, hallo, halli, hallo,
Da hat es keine Not.	There's nothing else I need.
Und streif' ich durch die Wälder	And when I roam the forests
Und zieh' ich durch die Felder	And walk across the meadows
Einsam den vollen Tag,	Alone the whole day long,
(Repeat line)	(Repeat line)
Dann schwinden mir die Stunden	Then pass the hours quickly
Gleich flüchtigen Sekunden,	Like seconds passing fleeting,
Tracht' ich dem Wilde nach.	While hunting game all day.
(Repeat line)	(Repeat line)
Halli, hallo, halli, hallo,	Halli, hallo, halli, hallo,
Tracht' ich dem Wilde nach.	While hunting game all day.

THE *Eintracht* (Concordia) Rifle Club meeting place in Gillespie Co. Such Groups and the choral clubs were the important bearers of the German song tradition.

—*Photo by the author, 1978.*

Wenn sich die Sonne neiget,
Der feuchte Nebel Steiget,
Mein Tagwerk ist getan.
(Repeat line)
Dann zieh' ich von der Heide
Zur häuslich stillen Freude,
Ein froher Jägersmann.
(Repeat line)
Halli, hallo, halli, hallo,
Ein froher Jägersmann.
(G.J.J.—See Schmidt, 100. NOTE: there are some slight variations and additional stanzas.)

And when the sun is setting,
The humid fog is rising,
My day's work has been done.
(Repeat line)
Then will I leave the meadow
And seek domestic pleasure,
A happy hunting man.
(Repeat line)
Halli, hallo, halli, hallo,
A happy hunting man.

9.

Below is one of the best songs of loneliness, expressing the displaced Germans' feeling of isolation in their new Texas home. Herr Wilhelm Lindemann of Comfort remembered this song from his earlier days as a choral singer, and he sang it to me from memory after he was over ninety years of age.

Verlassen, verlassen,
Verlassen bin i (ich),
Wie der Stein auf den Strassen
So verlassen bin i (ich).
Drum geh i (ich) zum Kirchlein
Zum Kirchlein weit draus,
Dort knie i (ich) mi (mich) nieder
Und wein' mi halt aus.
(W.L.)

Forsaken, forsaken,
Forsaken am I,
Like the stones in the pavement,
So forsaken am I.
For the church in the wildwood,
For the small church I'll start,
And I'll kneel down and weep there
And cry out my heart.

10.

Herr Lindemann also sang to me parts of the following song of yearning for his old *Vaterland*.

Nach der Heimat möcht' ich wieder,
Nach dem teuren Vaterort,
Wo man singt die frohen Lieder,

Wo man spricht ein trautes Wort.

Chor: Teure Heimat, sei gegrüsst,

In der Ferne sei gegrüsst,
Sei gegrüsst in weiter Ferne,
Teure Heimat, sei gegrüsst.

To my homeland I would wander,
To my precious home abroad,
Where they sing the songs out yonder,
Where they speak a kindly word.

Refrain: Precious homeland, hear my greeting
From afar, oh, hear my greeting,
Hear my greeting from afar,
Precious homeland, hear my greeting.

Deine Täler, deine Höhen,
Deiner heil'gen Wälder Grün,
O, die möcht' ich wieder sehen,
Dorthin, dorthin möcht' ich ziehn.
Chor: Teure Heimat, usw.

To your valleys, to your mountains,
To the sacred woods and trees,
Oh, these would I like to see,
That is where my fancy flees.
Refrain: Precious homeland, etc.

Doch mein Schicksal will es nimmer,
Durch die Welt ich wandern muss,
Trautes Heim, dein denk' ich immer,
Trautes Heim, dir gilt mein Gruss.
Chor: Teure Heimat, usw.
(W.L.)

But my destiny won't grant this;
Through the world I wander here.
Precious homeland, precious homeland,
Greetings to you, homeland, dear.
Refrain: Precious homeland, etc.

11.

Below is a beautiful song from Fredericksburg on the theme of young love.

Christina Philippina,
Komm mit mir ins Gras;
Da pfeifen die Vögel,
Da klappert der Has';
Wie hoch ist der Himmel,
Wie glanzen die Sterne,
Wie haben die Jungens
Die Mädchens so gerne!
(T.K.)

Christina Philippina,
Come with me in the grass;
There the birdies are piping,
For a rabbit and a lass.
How high are the heavens,
How the stars are shining,
How the boys love the girls
And for them are pining!

12.

The following is a song for a play-party game or a folk dance from Sisterdale. The boys and girls stand or march in a circle while one boy remains in the center. During the singing he chooses his partner. This continues until all the players have partners.

Es regnet auf der Brücke,
Und ich werde nass.
Ich hab' noch was vergessen
Und weiss nicht was.
Schöne Jungfrau, hübsch und fein,
Komm mit mir zum Tanz herein,
Lass uns einmal tanzen
Und lustig sein.
Lass uns einmal tanzen
Und lustig sein.
(A.W.P.)

It's raining on the bridges,
And I am getting wet.
I have forgotten something
And don't know what.
Pretty maiden, fine and fair,
Come with me the dance to share.
Let us dance a while
And jolly be;
Let us dance a while
And jolly be.

13.

Below is a love song of an entirely different nature from Fredericksburg. It is rustic and funny, expressing a sort of tongue-in-cheek longing for the dumb clod Christian, who is missed despite his hayseed personality.

Wo mag denn nur mein Christian sein,
In Hamburg oder Bremen?
Schau' ich nur seine Stube an,
Dann denk' ich an mein'n Christian.

Where, oh where could my Christian be,
In Hamburg or in Bremen?
When I but see his room or den,
Then I think of Christian.

In seiner Stub' da hängt ein Holz,
Damit hat er gedroschen.
Schau' ich nur diesen Flegel an,
Dann denk' ich an mein'n Christian.

In his room hangs a threshing cane;
With it he did his threshing.
When I but see this threshing cane,
Then I think of Christian.

Auf unserm Hof da steht ein Klotz,
Darauf hat er gesessen,
Schau' ich nur diesen Holzklotz an,
Dann denk' ich an mein'n Christian.

In our farmyard is a log;
Here he sat beside his dog.
When I but see this log again,
Then I think of Christian.

Der Esel, der den Milchkarr'n zog,
Den hat er selbst geführet.
Hör' ich nur diesen Esel schrei'n,
Denk' ich an mein Christian.

The donkey that our milk cart drew,
He drove him often and so true.
When I but hear this donkey scream,
Then I think of Christian.

In unserm Stall da steht 'ne Kuh,
Die hat er oft gemolken.
Schau' ich dieses Rindvieh an,
Dann denk' ich an mein'n Christian.
(E.W.K. & A.E.)

In our stable stands a cow;
Christian milked her oft till now.
When I but see this cow again,
Then I think of Christian.

14.

The *Doktor Eisenbart* (Doctor Ironbeard) folksong about the quack doctor is widely known in Texas and, of course, also in Germany. There are possibilities for many additions or stanzas, as the second one with its Houston and Texas-brags flavor shows. Any city name may be substituted.

Ich bin der Doktor Eisenbart,
Val-le-ral-le-ri, juch-hei!
Kurier' die Lent' nach meiner Art,
Val-le-ral-le-ri, juch-hei!
Kann machen, dass die Blinden geh'n,
Val-le-ral-le-ri, juch-hei-ras-sa!
Und dass die Lahmen wieder seh'n.
Val-le-ral-le-ri, juch-hei!
(D.A.J.—See also Bacon, *Vorwärts*, 123)

I am Doctor Ironbeard,
Val-le-ral-le-ri, juch-hei!
I cure all people, sound and weird,
Val-le-ral-le-ri, juch-hei!
I make the blind ones walk again,
Val-le-ral-le-ri, juch-hei-ras-sa.
And cause the lame to see again.
Val-le-ral-le-ri, juch-hei!

There is a second stanza in Bacon, but I will add the "hollow-tooth" stanza instead and use the "Jupei-di-heida" refrain, supplied by A.E.

In Houston kannt' ich einen Mann,
Jupei-di-heida,
Der hatte einen hohlen Zahn,
Jupei-di-heida,
Ich schoss ihn 'raus mit der Pistol',
Jupei-di-heida.
Ach Gott, wie ist dem Mann so wohl,
Jupei-di-heida.
(A.E., R.H., E.W.K.)

In Houston once a man I knew,
Jupei-di-heida,
He had a hollow tooth to shew,
Jupei-di-heida,
I took my pistol, shot it out,
Jupei-di-heida,
My God, he's well enough to shout,
Jupei-di-heida.

15.

The *Herr Schmidt* song, although basically German, also has a natural appeal for Texans. It accompanies a play-party game or a sort of folk dance. It is a delightful courting song. Boys and girls pair off and stand in lines facing each other, boys on one side and girls on the other. While the *Herr Schmidt* lines are sung, the first couple steps forward and does a little hopping step, clasping both hands, kicking forward first the right foot and resting on its heel, and then the left; and then for each "Herr Schmidt" phrase and for the rest of the couplet the dancers kick their feet back and forth to the rhythm of the music. Then while the second couplet is sung, the dancers skip to the other end of the lines, and the whole thing is repeated by the second couple, and so on.

Herr Schmidt, Herr Schmidt,
Wir haben eine Bitt'.
(Repeat couplet)
Auf Freiersfüssen kommen wir,
Man sagt, es sind viel Töchter hier.

Herr Schmidt, Herr Schmidt,
We want to talk a bit.
(Repeat couplet)
We come a courting, do not fear,
They say you have some daughters here.

Ja, ja, ja, ja,
Ich bin der Herr Papa!
(Repeat couplet)
Ein Dutzend Mädchen hab' ich nur,
Von jedem Jahrgang eine Spur.

Yes, yes, yes, yes,
I am their pa; no longer guess.
(Repeat couplet)
I have a dozen girls, you'll see,
A yearly vintage, fair and free.

Herr Schmidt, Herr Schmidt
Was kreigt denn Julchen mit?
(Repeat couplet)
Ein Schleier und ein Federhut,
Die steh'n dem Mädel gar zu gut.

Herr Schmidt, Herr Schmidt,
What will your Julie get?
(Repeat couplet)
A veil and feather hat, so fine,
They'll make that gal look good and shine.

Herr Schmidt, Herr Schmidt
Was Kriegt denn Dörchen' mit?
(Repeat couplet)
'ne Wiege und viel Kinderzeug,
Wenn's dann so weit ist, hat sie's gleich.

Herr Schmidt, Herr Schmidt
What will your Dora get?
(Repeat couplet)
A cradle and some kiddie clothes;
When you're that far, she'll get all those.

Herr Schmidt, Herr Schmidt,
Was kriegt denn Minchen mit?
(Repeat couplet)
Schön' Banderl und paar derbe Schuh;
Denn da passt ja das Mädel zu.

Herr Schmidt, Herr Schmidt,
What will your Minnie get?
(Repeat couplet)
Ribbons, gay, and heavy shoes;
That's what he'll get who this gal woos.

Herr Schmidt, Herr Schmidt,
Was kriegt denn Malchen mit?
(Repeat couplet)
Das Mädchen, das ist gut und brav;
Wer die kriegt, der hat ein Schaf.

Herr Schmidt, Herr Schmidt,
What will your Mollie get?
(Repeat couplet)
That gal is good and brave, I said;
Whoever gets her has a muttonhead.

Herr Schmidt, Herr Schmidt,
Was kriegt denn Lottchen mit?
(Repeat couplet)
Ein Envelopchen hübsch und fein
Und meinen Segen obendrein.

Herr Schmidt, Herr Schmidt
What will your Lottie get?
(Repeat couplet)
An envelope, all fair and fine,
All richly filled with blessings o'mine.

Herr Schmidt, Herr Schmidt,
Was kriegt denn Emma mit?
(Repeat couplet)
Den Schiller und den Walter Scott;
Denn Verse macht sie wie ein Gott.

Herr Schmidt, Herr Schmidt,
What will your Emma get?
(Repeat couplet)
The poets Schiller and Walter Scott;
Like God, she versifies a lot.

Herr Schmidt, Herr Schmidt,
Was bringt die Gusta mit?
(Repeat couplet)
Die Gusta ist für Sie kein Kraut;
Denn sie ist, Gott sei Dank, schon Braut.

Herr Schmidt, Herr Schmidt,
What will your Gusta get?
(Repeat couplet)
My Gusta is for you no game;
Thank God, she is betrothed and tame.

Herr Schmidt, Herr Schmidt,
Was bringt's Mariechen mit?
(Repeat couplet)
Der sieht man schon die dreissig an,
Da müssen meine Groschen dran.

Herr Schmidt, Herr Schmidt,
What will Mariechen get?
(Repeat couplet)
She shows she's thirty years or more;
I fear she'll make my shekels soar.

Herr Schmidt, Herr Schmidt,
Was bringt denn Luischen mit?
(Repeat couplet)

Herr Schmidt, Herr Schmidt,
What will Louisa get?
(Repeat couplet)

Das Mädchen sagt, sie heirat't nicht,	That gal, she says she'll never marry;
Doch daran stoss sich keiner nicht.	Don't worry, fellow, you can tarry.

Herr Schmidt, Herr Schmidt,	Herr Schmidt, Herr Schmidt,
Was bringt denn Elschen mit?	What will your Elsie get?
(Repeat couplet)	(Repeat couplet)
Die kriegt ein Sofa lang und breit	She'll get a sofa, long and wide,
Für ihre grosse Sittsamkeit.	Where her morals can abide.

Herr Schmidt, Herr Schmidt,	Herr Schmidt, Herr Schmidt,
Was bringt Rosalie mit?	What will Rosalie get?
(Repeat couplet)	(Repeat couplet)
Zwei Schinken und 'ne Kälberbrust;	Two hams and some veal brisket, too,
Denn Essen ist ja ihre Lust.	For eating is her pleasure, true.

Herr Schmidt, Herr Schmidt,	Herr Schmidt, Herr Schmidt,
Was bringt Ottilchen mit?	What will your Tillie get?
(Repeat couplet)	(Repeat couplet)
Ottilchen ist das Kuckucksnest,	My Tillie is the cuckoo's nest;
Die kriegt den ganzen Überrest.	She gets what's left, gets all the rest.
(W.L., A.E., & M.M.J.)	

16.

In Lauterbach hab' ich mein'n Strumpf verlorn,	In Lauterbach have I my stocking lost,
Und ohne Strumpf geh' ich nicht Heim;	And minus a sock can't go home;
Drum geh' ich wieder nach Lauterbach hin	I'll go right back to Lauterbach
Und kauf mir ein'n Strumpf an mein Bein.	And buy me a sock for to roam.
(G.J.J.)	(lit. for my leg).

There are several versions of the song, some in dialect, including the one in Schmidt, 120, with musical notes:

Z' Lauterbach hab' ich mein Strumpf
verlorn,
Ohne Strumpf geh i net Hoam,
Geh i halt wieder auf Lauterbach,
Kauf mir an Strumpf an dem Aan
(Bein).

NOTE: The translation of the variant is the same as the above.

17.

The *Droben auf grüner Heide* (yonder on the green meadow) song is similar to the English song "Old McDonald had a Farm," inasmuch as it develops a long repetitive sequence that gains interest by speeding up the tempo toward the end. the rythmic and rhyming words *Nest am Quast, Quast am Ast, Ast am Baum* (Nest on twig, twig on limb, limb on tree) add much to the appeal of the song to children. There are similar versions current in Germany.

The song begins with the refrain and then proceeds in a question and answer form and then repeats the items in reverse order.

Droben auf grüner Heide	Yonder on the green meadow
Steht ein Birnbaum, trägt Laub.	Stands a pear tree, bearing leaves.
Was ist denn an dem Baum?	And what is on the tree?
Ein wunderschöner Ast.	A very pretty limb.
Ast am Baum, Baum in der Erd';	Limb on tree, tree on the earth;
Droben auf grüner Heide	Yonder on the green meadow
Steht ein Birnbaum, trägt Laub.	Stands a pear tree, bearing leaves.
Was ist denn an dem Ast?	And what is on the limb?
Ein wunderschöner Quast.	A very pretty twig.
Quast am Ast, Ast am Baum,	Twig on limb, limb on tree,
Baum in der Erd';	Tree on the earth;
Droben auf grüner Heide	Yonder on the green meadow

Steht ein Birnbaum, trägt Laub.	Stands a pear tree, bearing leaves.
Was ist denn an dem Quast?	And what is on the twig?
Ein wunderschönes Nest.	A very pretty nest.
Nest am Quast, Quast am Ast,	Nest on twig, twig on limb,
Ast am Baum, Baum in der Erd';	Limb on tree, tree on the earth;
Droben auf grüner Heide	Yonder on the green meadow
Steht ein Birnbaum, trägt Laub.	Stands a pear tree, bearing leaves.
Was ist denn in dem Nest?	And what is in the nest?
Ein wunderschönes Ei.	A very pretty egg.
Ei im Nest, Nest am Quast,	Egg in nest, nest on twig,
Quast am Ast, Ast am Baum,	Twig on limb, limb on tree,
Baum in der Erd';	Tree on the earth;
Droben auf grüner Heide	Yonder on the green meadow
Steht ein Birnbaum, trägt Laub.	Stands a pear tree, bearing leaves.
Was ist denn in dem Ei?	And what is in the egg?
Ein wunderschönes Dotter.	A very pretty yolk.
Dotter im Ei, Ei im Nest,	Yolk in egg, egg in nest,
Nest am Quast, Quast am Ast,	Nest on twig, twig on limb,
Ast am Baum, Baum in der Erd';	Limb on tree, tree on the earth;
Droben auf grüner Heide	Yonder on the green meadow
Steht ein Birnbaum, trägt Laub.	Stands a pear tree, bearing leaves.
Was ist denn in dem Dotter?	And what is in the yolk?
Ein wunderschöner Vogel.	A very pretty bird.
Vogel im Dotter, Dotter im Ei,	Bird in yolk, yolk in egg,
Ei im Nest, Nest am Quast,	Egg in nest, nest on twig,
Quast am Ast, Ast am Baum,	Twig on limb, limb on tree,
Baum in der Erd';	Tree on the earth;
Droben auf grüner Heide	Yonder on the green meadow
Steht ein Birnbaum trägt Laub.	Stands a pear tree, bearing leaves.

(G.J.J. & D.J.—My father Daniel Jordan, Sr., sang this song to his children.)

17.

The *Butterblume* (Buttercup) song-poem has an appealing rural flavor with its flowers and sheep. It might well be a Texas song, and I would like to call it a Sisterdale poem, but I have no clear evidence of its origin.

Ach wär' ich eine Butterblume	Oh, if I were a buttercup
Und säss' im grünen Gras,	And sat in the green, green grass,
Dann frässen mich die Schäfelein,	Then little sheep would eat me up;
Das wär' ein rechter Spass.	What fun for a little lass!

(I.I.P.)

From the above songs we can see how and what the German-Texans sang, both in their singing societies and at home. In the next section some of the familiar drinking songs will be presented. They, like the songs above, belong to the tradition of convivial singing in Texas.

SHINER beer, Spoetzl Brewery at Shiner in the Texas German Belt.

9.

DRINKING SONGS

The drinking-song tradition is found throughout Germany, but it is particularly prominent in Bavaria and the South, where beer is the favorite beverage. But also in the wine-producing regions of the Rhine, Main, and Mosel river valleys, as well as in other regions, the people are fond of their drinking songs. The custom of singing beer-hall and wine-cellar songs, as well as the songs themselves were easily transplanted to Texas by the German colonists. After a slight slowdown during the prohibition years, they have been revived and preserved to the present day, and several newer songs were added in the 1930's. During the time when the communities in Texas held local-option or wet-dry elections, the German settlements could easily be spotted by the availability of beer and wine. It is largely these communities that perpetuated the drinking songs in Texas, thus making the song tradition in Texas similar to the one in Germany.

The only German-Texans opposed to beer drinking and later to all alcoholic beverages were the German Methodists. In the earlier days in Texas most of the people made their own wine from Mustang grapes, but beer was always more or less taboo among the German Methodists. During the Volstead Act era after 1919 they became staunch prohibitionists.

Below are a number of specimens of the German drinking songs sung in Texas.

Trink, trink, Brüderlein, trink,
Lass doch die Sorgen zu Haus!
Trink, trink, Brüderlein, trink,
Zeih deine Stirn nicht so kraus.
Meide den Kummer und meide den Schmerz,
Dann ist das Leben ein Scherz!
(Repeat last 2 lines)
(M.M.J. & C.E.S.)

Drink, drink, Brother, dear, drink;
Leave all your worries at home;
Drink, drink, Brother, dear, drink;
Don't wrinkle your forehead so glum.
Avoid all worry, avoid all pain,

Then you will your fun regain.
(Repeat last 2 lines)

2.

Bier her, Bier her
Oder ich fall um;
(Repeat first 2 lines)
Soll das Bier im Keller liegen,
Und ich hier die Ohnmacht kriegen?
Bier her, Bier her,
Oder ich fall um.
(H.W.)

Beer here, beer here,
Or I will drop dead;
(Repeat first 2 lines)
Shall the beer in cellars lie,
While I languish here and die?
Beer here, beer here,
Or I will drop dead.

3.

Wer soll das bezahlen?
Wer hat das bestellt?
Wer hat soviel Pinke-Panke?
Wer hat soviel Geld?
(W.L.)

Who shall pay for that?
Who has ordered that?
Who has so much funny money?
Who has so much flat?

4.

The next two songs (Nos. 4 and 5) are sung as toasts to someone on convivial occasions:

Hoch soll er leben,
Hoch soll er leben,
Dreimal hoch!
(Repeat all three lines)
(M.L.—Bacon *Vorwärts, 127.*)

Long (lit., high) may he live,
Long may he live,
Three times long.
(Repeat all three lines)

5.

The following song is also sung for toasting someone. It is related to No. 4 and may be sung in its place or in connection with it:

Er lebe hoch
(Repeat 4 times)
Hoch, hoch, hoch
Er lebe hoch!
(W.L.—Schmidt, 119.)

May he live long (lit., high)
(Repeat 4 times)
Long, long, long,
May he live long!

6.

One of the newer songs brought to Texas is the familiar *Hofbräuhaus* (Royal Brewery) song, that is sung not only in *München* (Munich), Germany, but also in Texas.

In München steht ein Hofbräuhaus,	In Munich stands a court-brew-house,
Eins, zwei, g'suffa.	One, two, now guzzle.
Da läuft so manches Fässchen aus,	There many a barrel is emptied out,
Eins, zwei, g'suffa.	One, two, now guzzle.
Da hat schon mancher brave Mann,	There many a good and honest man,
Eins, zwei, g'suffa,	One, two, now guzzle,
Gezeigt, was er vertragen kann.	Has showed how much he always can.
Schon früh am Morgen fing er an	In early morning his drinking began,
Und spät am Abend kam er heraus,	And late at night he finally came out,
So schön ist's im Hofbräuhaus.	So nice it's in the court-brew-house.
(T.T.)	

7.

Trink man noch ein Tröpfchen (Just drink another droplet) is a long and popular drinking song. It lends itself to endless and comical improvisations. Here is the stanza dealing with drinking:

Trink man noch ein Tröpfchen,	Just drink another droplet,
Trink man noch ein Tröpfchen,	Just drink another droplet
Aus dem kleinen Henkeltöpfchen.	From the little mug with a handle.
(Repeat the first three lines)	(Repeat the first three lines)
O Susanna,	Oh, Suzanna,
Wie ist as Leben doch so schön,	How very beautiful is life,
O Susanna, wie ist das Leben schön.	Oh, Suzanna how beautiful is life.

Then the song shifts to a series of stanzas whose chief theme, in figurative language, is "Everybody is doing it now, except some innocent teenager or some poor little impotent creature."

Alle Möpse bellen,	All the dogs are barking,
Alle Möpse bellen,	All the dogs are barking,
Bloss der kleine Rollmops nicht.	Only not the little hot dog.
(Repeat the first three lines)	(Repeat the first three lines)
O Susanna,	Oh, Suzanna,
Wie ist das Leben doch so schön,	How very beautiful is life,
O Susanna, wie ist das Leben schön,	Oh Suzanna, how beautiful is life.

The pun is in the *Rollmops*, which contains the word *Mops*, meaning *dog*, but it is the word for a herring stuffed with a pickle. I chose the word *hotdog*, which serves the dog pattern perfectly. Similar problems occur in the *Billy goat* lines, and I chose *wood goat* although the word *Holzbock* means *tick*. In the line about the *fish*, I used the words *teen age fish*, although I lost the reference to *girl*, and so on. Here are some of the other lines:

Alle Böcke stossen,	Billy goats are butting,
Nur der kleine Holzbock nicht.	Only not the little wood goat.
Alle Fische schwimmen,	All the fish are swimming,
Bloss der kleine Backfisch nicht.	Only not the little teen age fish (girl).
Alle Leute tanzen,	All the people are dancing,
Bloss der kleine [insert name] *nicht.*	Only little [insert name] not.
Alle Metzger metzen,	All the butchers are butchering,
Bloss der kleine [insert name] *nicht.*	Only little [insert name] not.

and so it goes on *ad infinitum* through a long series of "All the farmers farm," "All the Danz' dance," etc.

(T.K.—Schmidt, 121.)

8.

Lauter schöne Leut' sind wir,	None but pretty folk are we,
Leut' sind wir, Leut' sind wir,	Folk are we, folk are we,
Lauter schöne Leut' sind wir,	None but pretty folk are we,
Lauter schöne Leut'.	None but pretty folk.
Wenn wir schöne Leut' nicht wär'n,	If we pretty folk weren't here,
Wer tät' all das Bier verzehrn?	Who would drink up all the beer?
Lauter schöne Leut' sind wir,	None but pretty folk are we,
Lauter schöne Leut'.	None but pretty folk.

(T.K.)

9.

The *Schnitzelbank* (Wood carver's bench) song below is well suited for drinking bouts. It seems to be better known in the U.S.A. than in Germany, especially in Milwaukee, Wisconsin, where it gained great popularity through a widely distributed chart containing the words, pictures, and treble notes of the song. The charts were distributed by Mader's Restaurant in many places, including Texas, where the Pearl Brewing Company of San Antonio issued a card that is virtually a replica of the Milwaukee chart. The illustrated sheets were reprinted later by Jim Ethridge of Houston.

There are many verses in the printed versions. The Mader's chart and the Pearl Brewery card contain seventeen items each, and Curt Schmidt in his *Oma & Opa* book printed two illustrated versions with twelve and sixteen rhyming items respectively (Pp. 124-125). All these versions include notes for singing in unison. The song lends itself to impromptu additions, and the quality of the improvisations depends upon the state of inebriation of the composer.

Every stanza begins with a solo line in the form of a question, like *Ist das nicht eine Schnitzelbank,* and the response by the entire group: *Ja, das ist eine Schnitzelbank* (Is that not a carver's bench—yes that is a carver's bench). As items are added, the whole series is repeated each time, as in "The Twelve Nights of Christmas." To assist the slightly tipsy singers in remembering all the items and their sequence, the song leader or solo singer can point to the sheet with the illustrations. At the end of each stanza comes an end refrain, like *O, du Schönheit an der Wand; ja, das ist eine Schnitzelbank* (Oh you beauty on the wall; yes, that is a carver's bench). The "beauty on the wall" is a "wall flower," or the girl sitting by the wall waiting to be invited to dance. To make a rhyme with *bench* I translate the *Schönheit* line: "Oh, you pretty little wench." This singing and the addition of items can go on until the singers are exhausted and out of breath. Only six stanzas are printed in their entirety below, and then follows a list of additional items.

THE *Schnitzelbank* (Carver's Bench) song chart, with some of the typical scketches and musical notes, plus instructions for singing.
—*With permission of The Jim Ethridge Co., Houston*

Solo:
Ist das nicht eine Schnitzelbank?
Chor:
Ja, das ist eine Schnitzelbank.
O, du Schönheit an der Wand,
Ja, das ist eine Schnitzelbank.
Solo:
Ist das nicht ein Kurz und Lang?

Chor:
Ja, das ist ein Kurz und Lang,
Schnitzelbank, Kurz und Lang.
O, du Schönheit an der Wand,
Ja, das ist eine Schnitzelbank.
Solo:
Ist das nicht ein Kreuz und Quer?

Chor:
Ja, das ist ein Kreuz and Quer.
Schnitzelbank, Kurz und Lang,
Kreuz und Quer.
O, du Schönheit an der Wand,
Ja, das ist eine Schnitzelbank.
Solo:
Ist das nicht ein Schiessgewehr?
Chor:
Ja, das ist ein Schiessgewehr.
Schnitzelbank, Kurz und Lang,
Kreuz und Quer, Schiessgewehr.
O, du Schönheit an der Wand,
Ja, das ist eine Schnitzelbank.
Solo:
Ist das nicht ein Krumm und Grad?

Chor:
Ja, das ist ein Krumm und Grad.
Schnitzelbank, Kurz und Lang,
Kreuz und Quer, Schiessgewehr,
Krumm und Grad.
O, du Schönheit an der Wand,
Ja, das ist eine Schnitzelbank.

Solo:
Is that not a carver's bench?
Chorus:
Yes, that is a carver's bench.
Oh, you pretty little wench,
Yes, that is a carver's bench.
Solo:
Is that not a monkey wrench
(lit., short and long)?
Chorus:
Yes, that is a monkey wrench.
Carver's bench, monkey wrench,
Oh, you pretty little wench,
Yes, that is a carver's bench.
Solo:
Is that not a funny horse? (Actually a saw horse with criss-crossed legs.)
Chorus:
Yes, that is a funny horse.
Carver's bench, monkey wrench,
Funny horse.
Oh, you pretty little wench,
Yes, that is a carver's bench.
Solo:
Is that not a blunderbuss?
Chorus:
Yes, that is a blunderbuss.
Carver's bench, monkey wrench,
Funny horse, blunderbuss.
Oh, you pretty little wench,
Yes, that is a carver's bench.
Solo:
Is that not a crooked deal? (Lit. crooked and straight)
Chorus:
Yes, that is a crooked deal.
Carver's bench, monkey wrench,
Funny horse, blunderbuss,
Crooked deal.
Oh, you pretty little wench,
Yes, that is a carver's bench.

Solo:
Ist das nicht ein Wagenrad?
Chor:
Ja, das ist ein Wagenrad.
Schnitzelbank, Kurz und Lang,
Kreuz und Quer, Schiessgewehr,
Krumm und Grad, Wagenrad.
O, du Schönheit an der Wand,
Ja, das ist eine Schnitzelbank.

Solo:
Is that not a wagon wheel?
Chorus:
Yes, that is a wagon wheel.
Carver's bench, monkey wrench,
Funny horse, blunderbuss,
Crooked deal, wagon wheel.
Oh, you pretty little wench,
Yes that is a carver's bench.

And so it goes on as long as the singers' breath holds out. If the solo leader wants to end the whole thing, he speeds up the tempo until the singers fall out. Here are some extra items from the printed lists.

Grosses Glas, Ochsenblas	Big glass, ox bladder,
Haufen Mist, Schnickelfritz	Heap o' dung, snigger Fritz,
Dicke Frau, fette Sau	Corpulent woman, fat sow,
Quer und Rund, langer Hund	Across and around, long hound,
Dumme Gans, Affenschwanz	Silly goose, monkey tail,
Graue Katz, dumme Fratz	Gray cat, stupid face,
Regenschirm, Kirchenturm	Umbrella, church tower.

(E.G. & T.K.—Schmidt, 124-125.)

10.

Im Himmel gibt's kein Bier,
Drum trinken wir es hier.
Und sind wir nicht mehr hier,
Dann trinken die andern unser Bier.
(H.W.)

In heaven there is no beer,
That's why we drink it here.
And when we're gone from here,
The others will drink our beer.

With the increased popularity of alcoholic beverages in recent decades the drinking-song tradition has gained even more favor than it had earlier in the German-Texan communities, and it certainly is one of the major features of the German heritage in Texas.

10.

HUMOROUS POEMS AND LIGHT VERSE

Germans are not generally known for their sense of humor, partly because their serious bent of mind so often overshadows the humorous element. Nevertheless, there is a sizable body of whimsical and jocular literature in Germany, such as the hilariously funny and roguish books by Wilhelm Busch, like *Max und Moritz,* from which our own *Katzenjammer-Kids* comic strip developed; Doctor Heinrich Hoffmann's illustrated *Struwelpeter* (Slovenly Peter); the Ludwig Thoma stories and plays, like the *Lausbubengeschichten* (Stories About Mischievous Kids); the comical folk tales about *Die Schildbürger* (The People of Schilda); the prankish *Till Eulenspiegel* tales; the boastful Baron von Münchhausen stories; and humorous verse by Christian Morgenstern, among others. From these and other examples it can be seen that humorous literature is indeed found in many places and in various forms in Germany.

Some of the books cited above are by well known authors, but others are folkloric, somewhat related in spirit to the poems and light verse included in the present chapter. Most of these ditties were brought to Texas by the immigrants, and others have internal evidence that points to Texas as the place of origin. Suffice it to say that they are genuine German Texana and they are so well known that they were quoted from memory by my informants.

1.

Wie weh tut mein Finger, My finger is hurting,
Wie weh tut mein Fuss, My foot is in pain,
Wie weh tut mir alles, I hurt all over,
Wenn ich arbeiten muss. When I work again.

Es tut mir kein Finger, No finger is hurting,
Kein Fuss tut mir weh, No foot is in pain,
Wenn zum Tanzen, zum Springen, When I go dancing,
Zum Spielen ich geh'. And playing again.
(A.B.B. & W.J.I.)

2.

Regen, Regentropfen,
Die Jungen muss man klopfen;
Die Mädchen muss man schonen
Wie die Zitronen.
(J.H.K.)

Rain and raindrops, fleeting,
The boys will need a beating;
To girls you must be tender,
And they'll be sweet and slender.

3.

Sauerkraut und Rüben,
Die haben much vertrieben,
Hätt' meine Mutter Fleisch gekocht,

Dann wär' ich bei ihr geblieben.
(R.H.)

Sauerkraut and beets each day
Drove me from my home away;
If Mother had cooked me meat, somehow
I would have stayed at home till now.

Variations Line 3: *Hätte die Mutter...*
Line 4: *Wäre ich noch geblieben.*
(J.H.K.)

Translation of the variant is similar to the above.

4.

Wenn meine Mutter wüsste,
Wie es mir in der Ferne ging,
Tät' sie mir schicken a paar Hosen,
Wo nicht tät' der Wind durchblosen
[blasen].
(W.L.)

If my mother only knew
How things went for me abroad,
She would send me a pair of britches
With no wind holes, but good patches.

5.

Meine Hose hat ein'n Flicken,
Mein Hut hat ein Loch;
Brotscheiben gibt's keine dicken,
Aber lustig bin ich doch.
(D.A.J. & D.T.J.)

My britches have some patches,
My hat has a hole;
Our bread has no thick slices,
But I'm happy as a fool.

6.

Schuh' und Strümpfe sind zerrissen,
Durch die Hose pfeift der Wind.

Wenn das meine Mutter wüsste,
Wie's mir in der Fremde ging!
(D.A.J.)

Shoes and stockings, torn to pieces,
And the wind blows through my britches.
If my mother only knew,
How I missed her helpful stitches.

7.

Es regnet, es regnet,	It's raining, it's raining,
Es regnet seinen Lauf;	It's raining till it's done;
Und wenn's genug geregnet hat,	And when it's finished raining,
So hört's von selber auf.	It stops again on its own.
(G.J.J.)	

Variant:
So hört's auch wieder auf. Then it will stop again.
(W.J.I.)

8.

Du bist verrückt, mein Kind, You are crazy, my son,
Du musst nach Berlin, You must go to Berlin,
Dort wo die Verrückten sind, Where the crazy have gone,
Da gehörst du hin. That's where you'll fit in.
(T.K. & W.L.)

9.

Druch einen Ochsenstoss By a wild ox I was gored,
Flog ich in Abrahams Schoss; So to Abraham's bosom I soared;
Ich ging zur ewigen Ruh To eternal rest I flew
Durch dich, du Rindvieh du. Through you, dumb ox, through you.
(D.T.J.)

10.

Wasche dich, kämme dich, Wash yourself, comb your hair,
Putze dich fein; Make yourself gay;
Morgen soll deine Hochzeit sein. Tomorrow will be your wedding day.
(J.H.K.)

Variant:
Sonntag for *Morgen* Sunday for Tomorrow
(M.L)

11.

The following poem is a parody on the child's prayer *Ich bin klein, mein Herz ist rein* (I am small, my heart is pure).

Ich bin klein, I am small,
Mein Magen ist gross; My stomach is big;
Soll nichts hinein Shall nothing get in
Als Speck und Soss'. But gravy and pig (lit., bacon).
(D.A.J.)

12.

The next lines are very similar to a New Year's poem quoted above.

Wenn's Pfingsten ist, wenn's Pfingsten ist,	At Pentecost, at Pentecost,
Dann schlachtet der Papa ein'n Bock,	Our papa butchers a buck so wild;
Dann tanzt die Mama, dann tanzt die Mama,	Then Mama dances, then Mama dances,
Und fliegt der rote Rock.	And her red skirt twirls, my child.
(E.W.K. & E.G.)	

Variant has:
Vater and *Mutter* for Papa and Mama.
(L.P.)

13.

For some reason, unknown to me, Germans associate tailors with billy goats. This can be seen in Episode 3 of Wilhelm Busch's *Max und Moritz*. (Busch, III, 29-35.)

Wenn der Schneider reiten will	When the tailor wants to ride
Und hat kein Pferd,	And has no horse,
Dann setzt er sich auf ein'n Ziegenbock	He sits upon a billy goat
Und reit't verkehrt.	And rides in reverse.
(E.W.K.)	

A variant for line 3 reads:
Dann sattelt er sich ein'n Ziegenbock.	He saddles up a billy goat.
(G.J.J.)	

14.

Wenn Männer auseinandergehn,	When men take leave, they always try
Dann sagen sie: "Aufwiedersehn."	To say a final, quick "Goodbye."
Wenn Frauen auseinandergehn,	When women leave, they stand and talk
Dann bleiben sie noch lange stehn.	So long that I could take a walk.
(D.A.J.)	

15.

's ist mir alles eins, 's ist mir alles eins,	'Tis all the same to me, 'tis all the same to me
Ob ich Geld hab' oder keins.	Whether I have money or none, as it may be.

(Repeat)	(Repeat)
Wer ein Geld hat, der kann spekulieren,	Whoever has the money, he can speculate,
Und wer keins hat, der kann nichts verlieren.	But who has none, can but investigate.
's ist mir alles eins, ———	'Tis all the same to me, ———
Wer ein Geld hat, der kann Austern essen,	Whoever has the money can oysters eat each day;
Wer keins hat, kann Kartoffel fressen.	But who has none makes out on spuds, I say.
's ist mir alles eins, ———	'Tis all the same to me, ———
Wer ein Geld hat, der muss auch sterben,	Whoever has the money, he too must die some day;
Wer keins hat, muss schon so verderben.	And who has none must perish anyway.

(W.L., E.W.K.—See also Bacon *Vorwärts,* 128)

NOTE: There are several additional stanzas.

16.

Here we have another poem with grammatical errors; both are in the second stanza. The use of the accusative case *mich* for the dative *mir* is characteristic of Texas German. The second error is in the last line, this time the use of the nominative *wer* (who) for the accusative *wen* (whom). Since *wer* rhymes with *quer,* it seems that the correct *wen* form was not ever in the mind of the writer. These errors may be evidence that our copy is Texan because the practice of using *wer* for *wen* is extremely rare in Germany, whereas the use of *who* for *whom* is growing disconcertingly common in Texas and the U.S.A.

Mich ärgert die Fliege,	A fly and a flea
Mich ärgert der Floh,	Annoy me, oh woe!
Sie stechen mich beide,	They keep on biting me,
Doch weiss ich nicht wo.	But where, I don't know.
Mich [Mir] geht was im Kopf herum,	My head is all buzzing,
Die Kreuz und die Quer;	I don't know what to do;
Ich möcht' einen prügeln,	I'd like to beat someone,
Doch weiss ich nicht wer [wen].	But I don't know who [whom].

(D.T.J.)

17.

Mädchen, die pfeifen,
Und Hühner, die krähn,
Denen soll man bei Zeiten
Den Kragen (Kopf) umdrehn.
(D.T.J.)

Girls that whistle
And hens that crow,
Will always end
In trouble and woe.
(Lit., Their collars [heads] should be turned around.)

18.

Du bist wie der Schneider Puff;
Was du heute nähst, trennst du morgen wieder uf [auf].
(D.T.J.)

You are like tailor Pooh,
What today you sew, tomorrow you'll undo.

19.

Ja, so geht es in der Welt,
Der eine hat den Beutel,
Und der andre hat das Geld.
(W.J.I., E.G.)

In this world things are quite funny;
One fellow has the purse,
And another has the money.

20.

Lot ist tot, Lot ist tot;
Lieschen liegt am Sterben.
Das ist gut, das ist gut;
Jetzt gibt es was zu erben.
(M.M.J., T.K., & D.A.J.)

Lot is dead, Lot is dead;
Lisa is a goner, (lies dying).
That is good, that is good;
We'll get the inheritance sooner.

Variants: W.L. says any name will do in place of *Lieschen*. D.A.J. and D.T.J. say *Gretchen*.

21.

Die Juden haben ein Schwein geschlach't
Auf dem Tempel von Moses,
Und dann haben sie Wurst gemacht.

Ist das nicht was Kurioses?
(V.L.)

The Jews once killed a hog, so rare,
At the temple of Moses,
And then they made some sausage there.
Isn't that something curious?

22.

Weisst du was,
Wenn's regnet, ist's nass.
(G.J.J., M.L.)

You know what,
When it rains, it's wet.

The next group of poems are parodies on familiar songs. They seem to be especially popular in the Fredericksburg area, but I also heard some in Mason County.

23.
The following verse is a parody on *O du lieber Augustin*.

O, es sitzt 'ne Fliege an der Wand,
Fliege an der Wand, Fliege an der Wand,
O, es sitzt 'ne Fliege an der Wand.
Fliege an der Wand.

Oh, there sits a fly on the wall,
Fly on the wall, fly on the wall,
Oh, there sits a fly on the wall,
Fly on the wall.

O, wenn die Wand nicht wär',
Wand nicht wär', Wand nicht wär',
O, wenn die Wand nicht wär',
So wär' die Fliege auch nicht mehr.

Oh, if there were no wall,
Were no wall, were no wall,
Oh, if there were no wall,
There'd be no fly at all.

O es sitzt ein Aff auf dem Dach,
Aff auf dem Dach, Aff auf dem Dach,
O es sitzt ein Aff auf dem Dach,
Affe auf dem Dach.

Oh, there sits an ape on the roof,
Ape on the roof, ape on the roof,
Oh, there sits an ape on the roof,
Ape on the roof.

O wenn das Dach nicht wär',
Dach nicht wär', Dach nicht wär',
O wenn das Dach nicht wär',
So wär' der Affe auch nicht mehr.

Oh, if there were no roof,
Were no roof, were no roof,
Oh, if there were no roof,
There'd be no ape to goof (be no more ape).

(T.K.)

Variant: for *Fliege* in 1 and 2 is *Brummer*, short for *Brummfliege* (meat fly or blow fly.)
(D.A.J.)

24.
A parody on *O Tannenbaum* (Oh, Christmas Tree).

Das neue Lied, das neue Lied	A modern song, a modern song
Von dem besoffnen Wagenschmied.	About a drunken wheelwright man.
(Repeat both lines)	(Repeat both lines)
Wer das Lied nicht mehr weiter kann,	Whoever can sing on no more,
Der fängt es wieder von vorne an:	He starts again, just as before:
Das neue Lied, das neue Lied	A modern song, a modern song
Von dem desoffnen Wagenschmied.	About a drunken wheelwright man.

Die Fröschelein, die Fröschelein,	The little frogs, the little frogs,
Die haben keine Schwänzelein.	They have no tails, poor little frogs.
(Repeat both lines)	(Repeat both lines)
Wer das Lied nicht mehr weiter kann,	Whoever can go on no more,
Der fängt es wieder von vorne an:	He starts again, just as before:
Die Fröschelein, die Fröschelein,	The little frogs, the little frogs,
Die haben keine Schwänzelein.	They have no tails, poor little frogs.
(T.K.)

Variant: second stanza, lines 3 & 4:

Das ist ein gar zu lustig' Chor,	That is a very funny song;
Die haben ja auch keine Ohr'.	They have no ears; can't sing along.
(D.A.J. & D.T.J.)

Mein Vater hat's herausgebracht	My father found this out one day
Bei seiner letzten Konferenz,	While at a meeting far away:
(Repeat both lines)	(Repeat both lines)
Dass Frösche keine Haare hab'n,	That frogs don't have a coat of hair,
Und ebenso auch keine Schwänz'.	Their skins are rough and very bare.
Die Fröschelein, die Fröschelein,	The little frogs, the little frogs,
Die haben keine Schwänzelein.	They have no tails, poor little frogs.
(D.A.J. & D.T.J.)

25.
Parody on *Freut euch des Lebens* (Relish Life's Pleasures)

Zwei Knaben gaben sich ein'n Kuss;	Two boys gave each other a kiss;
Der eine, der hiess Julius;	The one was named Julius;
Der andre, der hiess Gretchen;	Gretchen was the other's name;
Ich glaube, das war ein Mädchen.	I think that was a gal or dame.
(M.M.J. & T.K.)

26.
Parody on *Schlaf, Kindchen, schlaf* (Sleep, Baby, sleep)

Schlaf, Kindlein, schlaf! Sleep, Baby, sleep;
Der Vater ist ein Schaf; Your father is a sheep (muttonhead);
Die Mutter ist ein Trampeltier. Your mother is a clumsy lout.
Was kann das arme Kind dafür? The kid can't help it; only shout.
(T.K., M.M.J., & A.E.)

27.
Another parody on *Schlaf, Kindchen, schlaf* (Sleep, Baby, sleep)

Schlaf, Kindchen, schlaf! Sleep, Baby, sleep;
Deine Mutter ist ein Schaf. Your mother is a sheep (muttonhead).

Dein Vater ist ein Dusseltier; Your father is a drunken steer;
Der trinkt nun lieber zu viel Bier. He's always drinking too much beer.
(C.E.S.)

From the humorous poems and the light verse above we will turn next to nonsensical ditties and tongue twisters, which in some cases are closely related to the poems above.

A TYPICAL German beer coaster with the words: *Wohl bekomm's*—May it do (you) much good.

11.

NONSENSICAL DITTIES AND TONGUE TWISTERS

Drawing the line between humorous verse and nonsensical ditties is not always easy. A good case could be made, for example, for including *Wenn der Schneider reiten will* (When the Tailor Wants to Ride) under nonsensical ditties, but I chose to include it under humorous verse. Children are usually intrigued by the silly meaningless ditties, but adults, too, are not altogether immune to the charm of these verses. The incongruity of the words often provides a funny flavor. ——Read them and laugh, but do not hunt for hidden meanings or for symbolism. Following the nonsensical ditties, a few typical German-Texas tongue twisters are added below.

NONSENSICAL VERSE

1.

Jetzt geh' ich nach Haus	Now I go to the house
Und brat' mir 'ne Maus;	And fry me a mouse;
Tu' ich sie auf 'ne Gabel,	If I put her on a fork,
Schmeck sie miserabel;	She'll taste miserably stark;
Tu' ich sie auf ein Messer,	If I use a knife to get her,
So schmeckt sie 'n bisschen besser.	She will taste a little better. |//
(J.H.K. & H.W.)

2.

"*Heinerich, was machst du da?*"	"Henry, what are you doing there?"
"*Vater, ich studiere.*"	"Father, I am studying."
"*Heinerich, das kannst du nicht.*"	"Henry, you cannot do that."
"*Vater, ich probiere.*"	"Father, I'll be trying."

(W.L. & G.J.J.)

3.

Mein lieber Bruder Ärgerlich	My dear brother Sourpuss
Hat alles, was er will.	Has everything he wants.
Und was er hat, das will er nicht,	And what he has, he doesn't want;
Und was er will, das hat er nicht.	And what he wants, he doesn't have.
Mein lieber Bruder Ärgerlich	My dear brother Sourpuss
Hat alles, was er will.	Has everything he wants.
(B.C.S.)	

4.

Neunundneunzig Schneider	Ninety-nine tailors
Wiegen hundert Pfund;	Weigh a hundred pound;
Wenn sie das nicht wiegen,	And if they do not weigh that much,
Sind sie nicht gesund.	They are not well and sound.
(D.T.J.)	

5.

A, B, Aam,	A, B, indeed,
Die Geis läuft im Sam'n,	The goat is in the seed,
Im Samen läuft die Geis;	In the seed is the goat;
Die Suppe ist heiss,	The soup is so hot,
Heiss ist die Suppe,	So hot is the soup;
Die Kuh hat ein'n Schnuppe,	The cow has the croup,
Ein'n Schnuppe hat die Kuh;	The croup has the cow;
Aus Leder macht man Schuh',	From leather we make shoes,
Die Schuh' macht man aus Leder;	Shoes we make from leather;
Die Gans trägt 'ne Feder,	The goose wears a feather,
'ne Feder trägt die Gans;	Feathers wears the goose;
Der Fuchs hat ein'n Schwanz,	The fox's tail comes loose,
	(Literally: The fox has a tail.)
Ein'n Schwanz hat der Fuchs,	Loose comes the fox's tail;
Der Edelmann fährt in der Kutsch,	The nobleman drives his coach to jail,
	(Literally: "...rides in the coach").
In der Kutsche fährt der Edelman,	His coach drives the nobleman
Der brav peitschen kann.	And cracks his whip as best he can.
(I.I.P.)	

6.

Fritz, Stiegelitz, dein Vogel ist tot,	Fritz Stiegelitz, your birdie is dead,
Liegt unter der Bank und frisst kein Brot.	Lies under the bench and eats no bread.
(B.C.S.)	
Variant: *Liegt unter dem Baum . . .,*	Lies under the tree . . .
(G.J.J.)	

7.

Die Katzenserenade	Cat Serenade
Tier und Menschen schliefen feste,	Man and beast were sleeping soundly,
Selbst der Hauptprophete schlief,	Even major prophets slept,
Als ein Schwarm geschwänzter Gäste	When a bunch of long-tailed tomcats
Auf die höchsten Dächer stieg.	On the tallest roof tops crept.
In dem Vorsaal eines Reichen	In the rich man's vertibule
Stimmten sie ihr Liedchen an,	They began to howl and sing.
So ein Lied, das Stein' erweichen,	Such a song would melt a stone,
Menschen rasend machen kann,	And to humans madness bring.
Hinz,* des Murners* Schwiegervater,	Hank,* the father-in-law of Mourner,*
Schlug den Takt erbärmlich schön,	Struck up the tomcat's mournful song.
Und zwei abgelebte Kater	And two worn-out, raunchy tomcats
Quälten sich, ihm beizustehn.	Tried their best to sing along.
Endlich tanzen alle Katzen,	Finally all cats were dancing,
Poltern, lärmen, dass es kracht;	Tumbling, falling, till things broke,
Poltern, heulen, sprudeln, kratzen,	They were howling, clawing, prancing,
Bis der Herr vom Haus erwacht.	Till the master of the house awoke.
Dieser springt mit einem Prügel	And he grabs a stick and swings,
Rundherum im Saal herum	Into the room the stick he flings,
Und zerbricht dabei den Spiegel,	And he breaks the family mirror,
Schmeisst ein Dutzend Tassen um.	Hits a dozen cups and saucers,
Stolpernd über einige Späne,	Stumbles over beams in terror,
Stürzt im Fallen auf die Uhr	And he hits the clock in falling,
Und zerbricht dabei die Zähne—	Breaks his teeth in all this mauling—
Blinder Eifer schadet nur.	Naught but harm comes from such brawling.

(D.A.J. & A.E.)

*Hinz and Murner are names of cats.

*Hank and Mourner are names of cats.

8.

The following poem must be a German-Texan product, inasmuch as it uses a germanized English word, *gespellt* (spelled) as a rhyme word.

Kaum war ich acht Tage auf der Welt, | When I was barely one week in this world,
Da hab' ich schon das A,B,C, gespellt. | The entire alphabet I controlled.
Mein Vater sagt': "Hans, du bist gescheit; | My father said: "Hans, you are smart;
Du musst hinaus in die weite Welt." | Go to the wide world and make your start."

Variant: *Du musst hinaus in die Welt so weit.* | (Same translation)
Kaum war ich acht Tage in der Fremd', | But hardly one week away to roam,
Schrieb ich ein'n Brief um ein neues Hemd. | I wrote for a shirt from the folks at home.
Um das Postgeld zu ersparen, | To save the postage stamp and fare,
Hab' ich den Brief selbst heimgetragen. | I carried the letter myself out there.
(D.T.J.)

9.

A,B, Abt; / die Katze schnappt; | A,B, Caps; / The pussy cat snaps;
A,B,U; / Du dummer Esel du. | A,B,U, / You stupid jackass, you.
(J.H.K.)

10.

O Werner, eine Eule, | Oh, Werner, an owl
Eine Eule im Heu; | In the hay for you;
Leise, Erna; leise Erna, | Now, Erna, don't howl;
Eulen heulen: "Huh, Huh!" | Owls hoot: "Whoo, whoo!"
(A.B.B.)

11.

A,B,X; | A,B,X;
Ich kann (weiss) nix. | I know nix.
(D.A.J. & D.T.J.)

12.

Ich bin klein, du bist gross; | I am small, you are tall;
Der Weihnachtsmann hat ein Loch in der Hos'. | Santa has holes in his overall (lit., pants.)
(G.J.J. & F.J.)

13.

The next ditty has a Texas flavor; There is one English word used: *Pen*, and two Texas-German-Belt grammatical errors: *Nach die Katzen-Pen*, instead of *Nach der Katzen-Pen*, and *Mit die Schwänze*, instead of *Mit den Schwänzen*. This suggests an indigenous origin.

Wo gehst du hin?	Where are you going then?
Nach die Katzen-Pen,	To the kitten's pen.
Wo die Hunde	Where the dogs give wails
Mit die Schwänze bellen.	With their wagging tails.
(M.M.J.)	

14.

The following ditty seems to have originated as a spite verse ridiculing the Methodists, hopefully in good humor. It can easily backfire by substituting for *Methodist*: *Katholik* (Catholic), *Lutheraner* (Lutheran), or *Evangelisch* (Evangelical), but *Methodist* has the best rhyme and was probably the original.

Methodist, der du bist,	Methodist, who thou art,
Der die grossen Brocken frisst,	Thou who eateth the biggest part,
Und die kleinen liegen lässt.	And leaveth behind what is too short.
(M.M.J.)	

15.

Ich will dir mal was sagen,	I'll tell you something to brag on:
Ein Stück vom alten Wagen.	A piece of an old wagon.
Wenn die Räder ab sind,	When the wheels are off and gone,
Kann man nicht mehr jagen.	You can't drive on and on.
(J.H.K.)	

TONGUE TWISTERS

16.

Fischers Fritz fischt frische Fische;	Fisher's Fritz fishes fresh fish;
Frische Fische fischt Fischers Fritz.	Fresh fish fishes Fisher's Fritz.
(G.J.J.)	

17.

Wir Wascherweiber wollten wohl	We washer women would wash
Weisse Wäsche waschen,	White wash so wet and white,
Wenn wir nur wüssten, wo	If we would well know where
Warmes Waschwasser wär'.	Warm wash water were.
(A.E. & D.A.J.)	

18.

Der dicke Dietrich trug	The thick (lit. fat) Theodoric dragged (lit. carried)
Den dünnen Dietrich durch	The thin Theodoric through
Den dicken Dreck.	The thick, thick mud;
Da dankte der dünne Dietrich	Then the thin Theodoric thanked
Dem dicken Dietrich,	The thick Theodoric that
Dass er ihn durch	He dragged him through
Den dicken Dreck trug.	The thick, thick mud.
(T.K.)	

Variants: for *Dietrich* are *Teufel*, *Deibel*, or *Deifel* (all mean *devil*).
(T.K.)

19.

Der Potsdamer Postkutschputzer The Postdam postcoach polisher
Putzt den Postkutschkasten. Polishes the postcoach panels.
(J.H.K.)

20.

Der Metzger wetzt das Metzgermesser. The butcher whets the wet butcher knife.
(D.T.J.)

21.

Here is a sort of tongue twister in reverse. Older children told little kids that they could speak Latin. Then they spoke the lines so fast that the little ones could not understand and thought it was Latin.

Kuh lief ums Feld rum Cow ran round fair field
Und fiel aufs Ohr um. And fell down on ear drum.
(G.J.J.)

The humorous ditties and tongue twisters appearing in the present chapter form a sort of folk entertainment, and as such they have been preserved by oral tradition. Few or none ever found their way into print in Texas.

12.

PROVERBS, ADMONITIONS, AND PICTURESQUE EXPRESSIONS

Gute Sprüche, weise Lehren, Useful proverbs, wisdom, clear,
Muss man üben, nicht nur hören. Must we practice, not only hear.
(D.T.J.)

    Curt E. Schmidt, in his book *Oma & Opa: German-Texan Pioneers* (53-57), tells how vital the proverbs and aphorisms (German *Sprichwörter* and *Sprüche*) were for the German-Texan immigrants. Parents and elderly people quoted these "pointed and loaded little sayings" constantly, and the children were "thoroughly indoctrinated" by these strongly conservative teachings. Through this pedagogical purpose, the proverbs and the folk wisdom were transmitted to the young, and at the same time a rich treasure of folklore was preserved.

    Basically, German proverbs do not differ much from the English, but the German-Texans were much fonder of their little poetic treasures than were the Anglo settlers, and they took every opportunity to quote their favorite sayings for the edification of the young and for their own enjoyment.

    The abundance of German proverbs, even in Texas, is almost overwhelming, and I was faced with the task of selecting a limited number for the present chapter. Again I relied on my informants to help me choose the best proverbs, but the actual selections are my own. Other people would surely have made different choices, and for good reasons, but the task and the pleasure were mine, and here are my selections. The typical short proverbs are put first in this chapter, then follow the admonitions, and finally a few picturesque idiomatic expressions. All the items are arranged alphabetically within each category and numbered within each group.

PROVERBS (*Sprichwörter*)

1.

An Gottes Segen, ist alles gelegen.
(H.W.)

Everything depends on God's blessing.

2.

Arbeit macht das Leben süss.
(O.E.B. & A.W.P.)

Work makes life sweet.

Variant:
Arbeit macht das Leben süss,
Faulheit steift die Glieder.
(D.T.J.)

Work makes life sweet;
Laziness makes stiff your limbs.

A facetious variant of last line reads:
Faulheit stärkt die Glieder.
(D.T.J.)

Laziness strengthens your limbs.

3.

Arm oder reich,
Die Erde bedeckt sie alle gleich.
(I.I.P.)

Rich man or poor,
The earth will cover both for sure.

4.

Auf einem Hieb fällt kein Baum.
(A.E.)

No tree falls from one stroke of the ax.

5.

Beinah' ist nie genug;
Beinah' ist Selbstbetrug.
(D.T.J.)

Almost is never enough;
It's self deception and a bluff.

6.

Der Apfel fällt nicht weit vom Stamm.
(D.T.J.)

The apple falls not far from the tree trunk.

7.

Der beste Wille ist der feste Wille.
(W.J.I.)

The best will is the firm will.

8.

Der Herr muss selber sein ein Knecht, The master himself must work with might, (Lit., The master must himself be a servant)

Wenn er's im Haus will haben recht. If he would have his house run right.
(D.T.J.)

9.

Der Klügste gibt nach. The wisest one gives in.
(A.W.P. & E.W.J.)

10.

Der liebe Gott sorgt dafür, God sees to it Himself
Dass die Bäume nicht in den Himmel wachsen. That the trees don't grow into heaven.
(I.I.P.)

11.

Die Alten zum Rat; Old people are for counsel;
Die Jungen zur Tat. Young ones are for action.
(A.W.P. & I.I.P.)

12.

Eigenlob stinkt; andern Lob klingt. Self praise stinks; other's praise clinks (sings).
(J.H.K)

13.

Das Ei will oft klüger sein, The egg often claims to be smarter
Als die Henne. than the hen.
(A.E.)

14.

Ein gutes Gewissen A good conscience
Ist ein sanftes Ruhekissen. Is a soft, resting pillow.
(A.E.)

15.

Ein schlafender Fuchs fängt kein Huhn. A sleeping fox catches no hens.
(A.E.)

16.

Ein Spatz in der Hand ist besser A sparrow in hand is better
Als die Taube auf dem Dach. Than a pigeon on the roof.
(D.T.J. & H.W.)

17.

Eine Hand wäscht die andere.   One hand washes the other.
(A.W.P.)

18.

Einem geschenkten Gaul   You don't look
Sieht man nicht ins Maul.   a gift horse in the mouth.
(H.W.)

19.

Ein'n Vogel, der morgens singt,   A bird that sings in the morning
Holt abends die Katz.   Will be caught by a cat without warn-
(I.I.P.)   ing. (Lit., . . . in the evening.)

20.

Frisch gewagt ist halb gewonnen.   Well begun is half done.
(A.W.P.)

21.

Geteilter Schmerz ist halber Schmerz;   Shared pain is only half a pain;
Geteilte Freude ist doppelte Freude.   Shared joy is double joy.
(E.G.)

22.

Hat man Wahl, hat man Qual.   If you have a choice, you have misery.
(H.W.)

23.

Hat man was,   If you have something,
Dann hat man Sorgen;   You have to worry;
Hat man nichts,   If you have nothing,
Dann geht man borgen.   You go and borrow.
(A.L.)

24.

Hunger ist der beste Koch.   Hunger is the best cook.
(I.I.P. & O.E.B.)

25.

Keine Rose ohne Dornen.   No rose without thorns.
(W.J.I.)

26.

Kleine Mäuse haben auch Schwänze.   Little mice have tails, too.
(M.L.)

27.

Kommt man über den Hund,
Kommt man auch über den Schwanz.
(D.T.J.)

If you can jump over the dog,
You'll clear his tail too.

28.

Kommt Zeit, kommt Rat.
(I.I.P. & M.L.)

Comes time, comes counsel.
(Time brings wisdom.)

29.

Langes Fädchen, faules Mädchen.
(D.T.J.)

If a girl sews with too long a thread,
She's either lazy or a plain dumb-head.

30.

Lügen haben kurze Beine.
(W.J.I.)

Lies have short legs.

31.

Man soll den Tag nie
Vor dem Abend loben.
(I.I.P.)

You should never praise the day
Before evening has had its say.

32.

Märzenschnee tut Früchten weh.
(A.E.)

March with snow brings fruit trees woe.

33.

Mit dem Hute in der Hand
Kommt man durch das ganze Land.
(M.L.)

With your hat in your hand (with politeness)
You'll make out well in all the land.

34.

Mitgegangen, mitgefangen, mitgehangen.
(H.W.)

Ran around together, caught together, hanged together.

35.

Mit viel hält man Haus,
Mit wenig kommt man auch aus.
(A.L.)

For keeping house you need a lot,
But you make out on what you got.

36.

Morgen ist auch ein Tag.
(M.L.)

Tomorrow is another day.

37.

Morgen, morgen, nur nicht heute,
Sagen alle faulen Leute.
(W.J.I.)

Tomorrow, tomorrow, but not today,
Is what the lazy people say.

38.

Muss ist eine harte Nuss.
(A.W.P.)

Must is a hard nut. (It is hard to do something when you have to do it)

39.

Müssiggang ist aller Laster Anfang.
(C.E.S.)

Idleness is the start of all vice.

40.

Nach getaner Arbeit ist gut ruhen.
(E.W.J.)

After a completed task you can rest well.

41.

Nichts ist so fein gesponnen,

Es kommt doch endlich an die Sonnen.
(W.J.I.)

Nothing (no scheme) is so finely spun (planned),
It finally reaches the light of the sun.

42.

Nichts ist so traurig wie ein Mann,
Der alles will und der nichts kann.
(G.J.J.)

Nothing is so sad as a man,
Who wants to do everything, but can't do anything.

43.

Reden ist Silber; Schweigen ist Gold.
(W.J.I.)

Talk is silver; silence is gold.

44.

Spare in der Zeit, so hast du in der Not.
(H.W.)

Save your money in time, and you'll have some when there's need.

45.

Übung macht den Meister.
(W.J.I.)

Practice makes perfect (Lit., "the master").

46.

Undank ist der Welt Lohn.
(W.J.I.)

Ingratitude is the world's reward.

47.

Unrecht Gut gedeiht nicht.
(I.I.P.)

Ill gotten wealth will not thrive.

48.

Viele Hände machen schnell ein Ende.
(A.W.P.)

Many hands will finish a job quickly.

49.

Viele Hunde sind des Hasen Tod.
(M.L.)

Many dogs are the rabbit's death.

50.

Viele Köchinnen verderben den Brei.
(D.T.J.)

Many cooks spoil the broth.

51.

Was Hänschen nicht lernt,
Lernt Hans nimmermehr.
(A.W.P.)

What little Hans doesn't learn,
Big Hans will never learn.

52.

Was ich nicht weiss,
Macht mich nicht heiss.
(G.J.J.)
Variant: *Was man nicht weiss,*
Macht einen nicht heiss
(I.I.P.)

What I don't know
Won't bother me so.

What you don't know
Won't bother you so.

53.

Was sein muss, muss sein.
(W.L.)

What has to be, must be.

54.

Was vom Herzen Kommt,
Das geht zum Herzen.
(C.E.S.)

What comes from the heart
Reaches another heart.

55.

Wenn der Mensch verrückt wird,
Fängt's im Kopf (oben) an.
(D.J.)

When a person goes crazy,
It starts in his head (at the top).

56.

Wenn die Maus satt ist,
Schmeckt das Mehl bitter.
(O.E.B.)

When the mouse is full,
The flour tastes bitter.

57.

Wer andern eine Grube gräbt,
Fällt selbst hinein.
(E.W.J. & M.L.)

Who digs a pit to trap others
Falls in himself.

58.

Wer "A" sagt, muss auch "B" sagen.
(M.L.)

Whoever says "A" must also say "B."

59.

Wer das Kleine nicht ehrt,
Ist des Grossen nicht wert.
(D.T.J.)

Whoever does not esteem the small,
Is not worthy of the great at all.

60.

Wer den Eltern nicht gehorchen will,
Muss der Trommel gehorchen
(I.I.P.)

Whoever will not his parents obey
Must to the army be sent away (obey the drum).

61.

Wer einmal lügt, dem glaubt man nicht,
Und wenn er auch die Wahrheit spricht
(H.W. & W.J.I.)

Who once tells lies, men won't believe,
Though truthful he may speak and live.

62.

Wer gut schmiert, der gut fährt.
(E.D.)

Whoever greases well, he drives well.

63.

Wer lügt, der stiehlt auch.
(M.L.)

Whoever lies also steals.

64.

Wer seine Arbeit fleissig tut,
Dem schmeckt auch seine Suppe gut.
(D.T.J.)

Who diligently does his labor,
His soup will always have good flavor.

ADMONITIONS AND ADVICE.

1.

Den Kopf halt kühl, die Füsse warm,
Das macht den besten Doktor arm.

(G.J.J., as told by Emil Schuessler, Seguin.)

Your head keep cool, your feet keep warm,
That makes the doctors poor and squirm.

2.

Frage nicht, was andere machen;
Sieh auf deine eignen Sachen.
(D.T.J.)

Ask not what other people do;
See to your own and what's best for you.

3.

Gehe ohne Gottes Wort
Niemals aus deinem Hause fort.
(D.T.J.)

Without God's spirit and His word
Go never from your house abroad.

4.

Lerne was, so kannst du was.
(M.L.)

Learn something and you'll be able to do something.

5.

Mit Verwandten iss und lach',
Aber nie Geschäfte mach'.
(E.J.M.)

With relatives you laugh and dine,
But business deals don't make or sign.

6.

Mit Messer, Gabel, Schere und Licht
Spielen kleine Kinder nicht.
(D.T.J.)

With lamps and scissors, knife and fork,
Little children don't play or work.

7.

Nun gibt es wohl noch manche Sachen,
Wo man nicht weiss: wann, wie und wo.
Sieh zu, wie es die andern machen,
Und mach' es möglichst ebenso.
(D.T.J.)

There are so many things out yonder,
And you don't know when, how, or where.
See how the others act and ponder;
Then you can know how you will fare.

8.

Ordnung lerne, liebe sie; Learn good order, love it too,
Ordnung spart dir Zeit und Müh'. It saves time and trouble for you.
(W.J.I.)

9.

Quäle nie ein Tier zum Scherz, Never torture a beast for sport,
Denn es fühlt wie du den Schmerz. It feels, like you, the pain and smart.
(D.T.J.)

10.

Schuster, bleib bei deinen Leisten. Cobbler, stay with your shoemaker's
(W.L.) lasts.

11.

Verschiebe nie auf morgen, Never put off or delay
Was du heute kannst besorgen. Whatever you can do today.
(W.J.I.)
Variant:
Was du heute kannst besorgen, Whatever you can do today
Das verschiebe nicht auf morgen. Never put off or delay.
(D.T.J.)

12.

Was du nicht willst, das man dir tu', What you don't want others to do to you,
Das füg' auch keinem andern zu. That you should never to others do.
(A.W.P.)

PICTURESQUE EXPRESSIONS.

1.

1. *Der Junge hat kein Sitzfleisch.* The boy has no sitting flesh, i.e., The boy won't sit still and always wants to be on the move.
(G.J.J.)

2.

Die Frau hat die Hosen an. The wife is wearing the pants (is
(D.J.) boss).

3.

Die Frau hat Haare auf den Zähnen. The woman has hair over her teeth,
(D.J. & W.L.) i.e., The woman has a moustache,
  i.e., She is tough and rough like a man.

4.

Diese Leute leben aus der Hand in den Mund.
(D.J.)

These people live from hand to mouth.

5.

Er fällt mit der Tür ins Haus.
(O.M.)

He falls with the door into the house, i.e., He is blunt and bursts right out with everything.

6.

Er hat die Katze aus dem Sack gelassen.
(D.J. & M.L.)

He let the cat out of the bag.

7.

Er hat eine Katze im Sack gekauft.
(D.J.)

He bought a cat in a sack, i.e., He bought a pig in a poke.

8.

Er hat grosse Rosinen im Kopf.
(D.J. & M.L.)

He has big raisins in his head, i.e., He has wild plans in his head, or, He has his head in the clouds.

9.

Er hat sich einen kleinen Aff gekauft.
(C.E.S.)

He bought a little ape,

i.e., He is a bit tipsy.

10.

Er ist ein Schafskopf.
(M.L.)

He is a muttonhead, i.e. a dumbbell.

11.

Er ist noch nicht trocken hinter den Ohren.
(D.J.)

He isn't dry yet behind his ears,

i.e., He is young and inexperienced.

12.

Er setzt sich gerne zwischen zwei Stühle.
(D.J.)

He is inclined to sit down between two chairs,

i.e., He usually misses his boat.

	13.	
Er will das Gras wachsen hören. (I.I.P.)		He claims he can hear the grass grow, i.e., He is a "smart aleck."

	14.	
Er will Wasser in einem Sieb tragen. (H.W.)		He would carry water in a sieve, i.e., He always does things the wrong way.

	15.	
Es ist mir [alles] Wurst. (G.J.J.)		It's all sausage to me, i.e., It's all the same to me.

From the folk wisdom of the proverbs and admonitions and the picturesque folk expressions we go next to the section on riddles.

THE modern replica of the original Fredericksburg *Vereinskirche* used in the 19th century as church, school, and civic center.

135

13.

RIDDLES.

Riddles are a form of folk entertainment, but they are not uniformly known and preserved in all parts of the German Belt of Texas. There seems to be more interest in riddles in Fredericksburg than in New Braunfels, for example; and it is also clear from the responses of my informants that riddles now play a lesser role among German-Texans than do poems, ditties, verses, songs, and proverbs. This may be because my respondents were middle-aged and elderly people, and riddles do not hold the same attraction for these people as they do for young folks and children. This current lack of interest in riddles is all the more puzzling inasmuch as the little German school books used by these people prior to World War I contain a number of riddles that are apparently forgotten now by many people. Nevertheless, enough good riddles were reported as being currently known to make up the following group of selected riddles. Of course, there are others available and unreported; but the present specimens are adequate for a good sampling. The riddles are arranged alphabetically by their first words.

1.

Erst weiss wie Schnee,	First white as snow,
Dann grün wie Klee,	Then green as clover,
Dann rot wie Blut,	Then red as blood,
Schmeckt allen Kindern gut.	Tastes good all over.
Antwort: eine Kirsche oder eine Pflaume.	Answer: a cherry or a plum.

(D.A.J.)
Variant:

Dann schmeckt es gut.	Then it tastes good.

(R.H.)

2.

Es ist ein kleines, weisses Haus,	It is a tiny whitish house,
Hat nichts von Fenstern und von Toren;	Has neither doors nor windows;
Und will der kleine Gast heraus,	And if the little guest wants out,
So muss er erst die Wand durchboren.	He first must pierce the wall.
Antwort: Ein Ei.	Answer: An egg.
(D.A.J. & E.G.)	

3.

Einer kam gegangen; — A fellow came walking along,
Fünf haben ihn gefangen; — Five caught him doing wrong;
Sie brachten ihn nach Rippelbach, — They took him first to Ripplebrook,
Von Rippelbach nach Nagelbach, — From Ripplebrook to Fingernailbrook,
Da wurde er umgebracht. — And there they killed him for doing wrong.

Variant:
Und da blieb er hangen. — And there he was hanged (smashed) for doing wrong.

Antwort: *Ein Floh kam gegangen; Fünf Finger haben ihn gefangen und zwischen den Nägeln umgebracht.* — Answer: A flea came walking along, and five fingers caught him and crushed him between their nails.
(D.A.J. & D.T.J.)

Variant:
Es kamen zwei gagengen, — Two guys came walking along,
Die haben einen gefangen; — They caught another doing wrong;
Sie brachten ihn nach Rippelwitz, — They took him first to Middlewails,
Von Rippelwitz nach Nagelspitz, — From Middlewails to Fingernails,
Da haben sie ihn getötet. — And there they killed him for doing wrong.

Antwort: *Zwei Finger haben einen Floh gefangen und getötet. (umgebracht)* — Answer: Two fingers caught a flea and killed him at "Fingernails."
(J.H.K.)

4.

Es rüttelt sich — It makes a loud sound,
Und schüttelt sich — And shakes all around
Und macht ein'n Haufen — And underneath
Unter sich. — It makes a mound.
Antwort: Ein Mehlsieb. — Answer: A flour sieve.
(H.W. & W.L.)

14.

ANECDOTES AND JOKES

Anecdotes and jokes, like riddles, are a popular form of folk entertainment and they represent some of the best examples of indigenous Texan folklore. They are usually transmitted orally, and as a result there are several versions of some of the stories. Most of those included in the present chapter are based on misunderstandings between German and English speaking people, and the lack of perfect communication between the two ethnic groups.

As might be expected, the anecdotes seem especially humorous to bilingual speakers who may have had similar experiences. I well remember how in my first year in school some of the older boys laughed at me when I said "It's all *egal* to me" for "It's all the same to me." It does not take many such experiences for a bilingual child to mind his p's and q's and keep from talking what Germans call *Kauderwelsch* (gibberisch) or a mixture of several languages so common in bilingual communities.

1. A case in point here is the conversation between two old German-Texas hayseeds who were loading a wagon in the field. When the load got so high that the one on top of the wagon could not see the hay on the ground, he yelled: "Is de hay bald all" (meaning: Will the hay soon be all gone). The one below shouted: "Laang not." (Meaning in German: "Noch lange nicht," English: "Not by a long shot.") - (D.T.J.)

2. In Gillespie County, and elsewhere a number of tales are told about Sheriff Klaerner, the Elder, of Fredericksburg. These stories have become a generic type of joke that can also be told about other people for whom the tales fit. Two Klaerner jokes, Numbers 2 and 3, are included in the present chapter. The first one goes as follows:

On one occasion Sheriff Klaerner was in a San Antonio barbershop getting his semi-annual haircut. When the barber asked him: "Now, Herr Klaerner, won't you also have a manicure?" Klaerner replied without hesitation: "But *nein,* Ve already haf a *Männerchor* (male chorus) in Friedrichsburg." (D.T.J.)

DATE DUE			
MAR 25 1986		SEP -3 1987	
		APR 3 1991	
AUG 12 1986		AUG 1991	
		05/06/93	
JAN 15 1989		FEB 22 1994	
FEB 16 1989			